I0049371

ECONOMIC TERMITES

BUSINESS OWNERS: PROTECT YOUR
ASSETS FROM FINANCIAL DESTRUCTION

ROBERT WOLF

ECONOMIC TERMITES

Published by Wisdom House Books, Inc.
Chapel Hill, North Carolina 27514 USA
1.919.883.4669 | www.wisdomhousebooks.com

Wisdom House Books is committed to excellence in the publishing industry.

Book design copyright © 2019 by Wisdom House Books, Inc. All rights reserved.

Cover and Interior Design by Ted Ruybal

Published in the United States of America

Paperback ISBN: 978-1-7331877-0-1
LCCN: 2019911491

BUS098000 | BUSINESS & ECONOMICS / Knowledge Capital
BUSINESS & ECONOMICS / Money Management see Personal Finance /
Money Management
BUSINESS & ECONOMICS / Planning see Strategic Planning

First Edition

14 13 12 11 10 / 10 9 8 7 6 5 4 3 2 1

TABLE OF CONTENTS

INTRODUCTION

Do We Really Need Another Book on Finances?

Every time I read a new book on the topic of finance, I ask myself this same question. Yet, over the years, I realized there may not be *enough* books on this topic. So many opinions exist, and the search for answers is never-ending. People who need help become frustrated and don't know how to take all the information and apply it to their own situation. With this book, I want to move beyond mere opinions to give you *reasons* for why to handle or think about your finances in a certain way.

Throughout my career, I discovered the main concerns people had about financial topics were:

1) not receiving real answers or receiving answers based only on an expert's training and comfort level, and/or

2) not knowing how their plan works with their changing needs.

Being an avid reader, I studied ideas by investment, insurance, real estate, legal, tax professionals, and more. But I haven't found anyone connecting all of these ideas and simplifying our industry to an understandable level while speaking directly to people—without talking down to them or over them.

I want people like you to have an understanding about your money. I figured the best way to accomplish this was to educate others on money basics. So I decided to meet people where they are and found they're all pretty much in the same place—confused. In addition to no one connecting the available information to your specific situation, no one addressed how certain challenges affect the growth of your money.

Enter "Economic Termites." I woke up with this phrase in my head one night. The term seems rather baffling at first. I use it to help create a visual of how certain economic terms, processes, and events affect us. For our purposes here, we are more concerned about what they do rather than what they are. According to Orkin, a pest control company:

> *"Termites are often called the 'silent destroyer' because they may be secretly hiding and thriving in your home or yard without any immediate signs of damage."*[1]

Many events in our business and personal lives have "silent destroyers"—just like how termites can cause damage without us even knowing about it until it's too late. I began using this term while teaching the rules of money and how assets work. I figured if someone knew how their decisions would be affected due to these Economic Termites, and how the rules of assets worked, they could make different or more educated decisions.

As a result, I developed into a "personal CFO" for my clients. According to Investopedia,

> A chief financial officer (CFO) is the senior executive responsible for managing the financial actions of a company. The CFO's duties include tracking cash flow and financial planning as well as analyzing the company's financial strengths and weaknesses and proposing corrective actions.[2]

The common approach in the finance industry, one person manages an area of finance while someone else manages another portion. This leaves the client trying to figure out how to manage both. No wonder so many procrastinate.

Planning for your financial future is compartmentalized into three categories: family, business, and legacy and succession planning, respectively.

1) **Family Planning:** This consists of the traditional "financial planning," which includes trying to solve the "goals" and "dreams" of the family

and can address the budgeting, retirement, and college puzzles. This may include looking at stock market invesments and the incorporation of life insurance products. Some professionals do go beyond this to provide a comprehensive approach, but they're rare in my experience.

2) **Business Planning:** In this area, you either have the professional who sets up and manages the company retirement plan(s) or the life insurance professional who helps set up a Buy/Sell agreement or some sort of "executive carve out" for the business owner and, sometimes, key employees. The benefits broker and commercial insurance broker fit into this category.

3) **Legacy Planning:** This is linked to the Family Planning model and includes estate planning or preparation for the family wealth to be passed down to either the next generation and/or a charitable organization.

4) **Succession Planning:** A business owner does their due diligence with trying to pass the business to the next generation, sell it, or plan to exit the business effectively.

Family
Planning

Business
Planning

Legacy/
Succession
Planning

Each one of these areas affects the other.

This book focuses on business owners, which can involve a variety of scenarios. If I was too specific, it would do you a disservice, because you are different than your peers. To take those differences into account, I structured the book from a general holistic approach. From that, you can understand the methodology, language, and terminology we use in our planning. If we meet, we can get more specific about your situation with you already understanding our language or at least having exposure to it. This allows us to be more productive together and have your plans up and running sooner. If you are just looking for information and not a firm, then hopefully the information still helps. We have other resources to assist you, so please feel free to use them.

I've read hundreds of books over the years and most enjoyed the ones more technical in nature. Other times, I preferred books that told a story to convey a message. *Economic Termites* combines the two styles. Since we all learn and understand topics differently, I wanted to offer you, the reader, a choice. The first section uses terminology and examples to explain the terminology. I will talk about how we approach topics with our clients. In section two, I'll share the story of two brothers taking different approaches—one uses our service and one does not.

For more information about me please go to the back of this book or to our website www.terrafirmaconsultantsllc.com

After reading my book, if you would like more information please feel free to schedule a 30-minute strategy session.

SECTION ONE

CHAPTER ONE

The Beginning and Foundation

O ur goal is to *increase our client's cash flow,* and we do this by implementing our financial planning methods and strategies. We focus on our clients' cash flow since what they need, want, and desire are all based on that cash flow. This definition of cash flow[3] focuses on business. We strive to speak about your personal finances as a business, because you need to know your numbers to reach your dreams and goals. We'll explain this more throughout the book.

> *Cash flow is the net amount of cash and cash-equivalents being transferred into and out of a business. At the most fundamental level, a company's ability to create value for shareholders is determined by its ability to generate positive cash flows, or more specifically, maximize long-term free cash flow.*
>
> *Assessing the amounts, timing and uncertainty of*

cash flows is one of the most basic objectives of financial reporting. Understanding the cash flow statement– which reports operating cash flow, investing cash flow and financing cash flow—is essential for assessing a company's liquidity, flexibility and overall financial performance.

Positive cash flow indicates that a company's liquid assets are increasing, enabling it to settle debts, reinvest in its business, return money to shareholders, pay expenses and provide a buffer against future financial challenges. Companies with strong financial flexibility can take advantage of profitable investments. They also fare better in downturns by avoiding the costs of financial distress.

Even profitable companies can fail if operating activities do not generate enough cash to stay liquid. This can happen if profits are tied up in accounts receivable and inventory, or if a company spends too much on capital expenditure. Investors and creditors, therefore, want to know if the company has enough cash and cash-equivalents to settle short-term liabilities. To see if a company can meet its current liabilities with the cash it generates from operations, analysts look at debt service coverage ratios.

But liquidity only tells us so much. A company might have lots of cash because it is mortgaging its future *growth potential by selling off its long-term assets or taking on unsustainable levels of debt.*

To understand the true profitability of the business, analysts look at free cash flow(FCF). It is a really useful measure of financial performance – that tells a better story than net income — because it shows what money the company has leftover to expand the business or return to shareholders, after paying dividends, buying back stock or paying off debt

Yes, we could ask you about your goals and dreams. We could question you on what you want to do in five, ten, and twenty years, but why would I limit us that way? If you are coming to us, then I know you want to know the rules of assets and how to build, grow, and preserve your estate.

I want to help you shoot for the stars and hit the moon if we fall short. I don't want to shoot for just the clouds and have you hit a mountain. If we are your "personal CFO," then you don't need someone to coddle you or make things seem superficially rosy. At the start, we won't outline your hopes and dreams, because they're based on your current understanding as opposed to what we'll teach and show you what can be possible. This may sound harsh, yet it helps you in the long run. In short, *your CASH FLOW* is important because it is *YOUR money, YOUR hard work, and YOUR reward.*

You have heard the phrase "Cash is King." I'm going to go on record and say I disagree. Let me explain. You see if cash is sitting stagnant in a particular place doing nothing then it is unproductive and therefore really cannot be called and asset. Remember an asset is something that creates income.

So let me explain, have you ever gone on a walk and noticed a body of water whatever size, and it has algae growing, bugs flying around, and it has a poor odor. Why is that? Well it's because there is no movement, it's just sitting there, stagnant. But the moment there is flow of water into that same pool of water what begins to happen?

The bugs go away, the odor dissipates, an the algae begins to disappear. Why is that because the flow of water causes the stagnant water to move around. Now you may not go drink the water but you get the point of what happens.

Cash works the same way, when the flow of cash occurs then you have an asset. So the term cash is king should be the flow of cash is king.

Our Approach is to educate you on the rules of assets and how your money works. By educate,[4] we mean:

- to develop the faculties and powers of (a person) by teaching, instruction, or schooling,

- to qualify by instruction or training,

🐜 to provide schooling or training for,

🐜 to develop or train,

🐜 to inform.

We are hired to do what we do—not do what you think we should do. Why hire us? We are not "yes men." We are educators and work for you to educate you and consult with you while you always remain in charge of the decisions. In learning our methods, you'll have information to make an informed decision and know whether the consequences would be good or bad. Although our goal is to review all the information, certain circumstances—the Economic Termites we'll discuss later—may affect our knowledge base.

Outliers: The Story of Success

I am constantly asked what book someone should read to understand our planning method. Besides having a crazy brain that thinks like mine, you can go to our website to see a list of the books I have read over the years. This list does not include workshops, continuing education classes, articles, and other avenues of learning.

In 2011, I read a book called *Outliers: The Story of Success* by Malcolm Gladwell. (By the way I will be referencing books I have read throughout the years to try and help share what I've learned). In this book, he references stories of how people become successful. He mentions the "10,000 hour rule," which states that it takes 10,000 hours of training and practice to be an expert at something.

Robert Kiyosaki

When my wife and I were newly married, I read a book by Robert Kiyosaki called *Rich Dad Poor Dad*. He explained money and how the rules of money should be viewed. I liked his book so much that I bought a second one by him called *Cashflow Quadrant*. This book caused me to give my two-week notice and enter the financial world. I loved his explanation of what the different quadrants mean, so let's take a look at them now.

The first quadrant is the E Quadrant, which represents those who are employees. In this quadrant, you have a job and are trading time for dollars. You negotiate with an employer on your value to the company, and they are negotiating with you on what that value is worth to them.

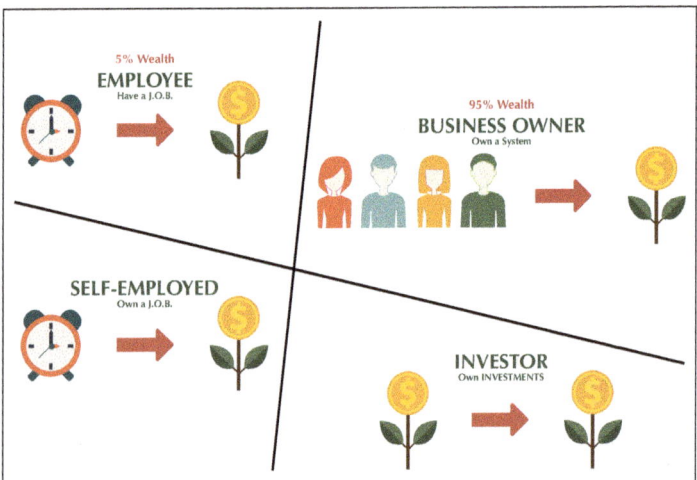

The two parties reach an agreement around when you get hired, what you're paid, and what benefits you receive. This situation results in one of the higher tax rates and is based on the individual income tax rates. The E quadrant is where you have personal tax rates. You can see on your Form 1040 that these are the most expensive tax rates under the tax code. Taxes will be discussed in more depth later.

The **S Quadrant** is named for those who are self-employed. In this quadrant, you work for yourself yet still trade time for dollars. You offer products or services to customers/clients based on the products or services your company provides. The customers/clients and you decide on the value based on their needs and what they are willing to pay. I'm not suggesting this is a negotiation or haggle. This happens as a byproduct of business because you need to change the price if clients aren't buying. In the "S" Quadrant, you're paying for your own benefits. This is also one of the higher tax rates based on the individual income tax rates under the federal tax Form 1040. As mentioned in the E quadrant, this quadrant has the same issue with high tax rate, yet you can deduct expenses. In this scenario, you also have to pay both employee and employer payroll taxes.

The **B Quadrant** represents business owners. In this quadrant, you have a system in place to generate revenue, and you have employees to help generate revenue.

Like the S Quadrant, this quadrant offers products or services to customers/clients based on the value of those products or services to the customers/clients. You decide on the value based on their needs.

Your system allows you to generate a more consistent revenue stream—or at least, that's the goal. Due to this, the IRS offers business incentives to increase revenue, so the business can hire employees. Why? Go back to the E Quadrant and re-read the taxation. It's one of the higher tax generators. The incentives that businesses receive are called tax deductions. Later, we'll talk more about the benefits of these and the different kinds, so you can see how you can build your assets. Since the IRS wants to encourage you to grow your business, this scenario offers the best tax advantages, so you can hire more employees (taxpayers).

The **I Quadrant** represents Investors. In our firm, we use the term "asset builder" instead. The word "investor" or "investments" calls to mind the stock market. We want to make sure you understand that we are referring to building assets, and we want you to accumulate and grow your assets. Before I continue, an asset[5] is:

> . . . anything of value or a resource of value that can be converted into cash. Individuals, companies, and governments own assets. For a company, an

asset might generate revenue or the company might benefit in some way from owning or using the asset.

Examples of personal assets include:

- Cash and cash equivalents, certificates of deposit, checking, and savings accounts, money market accounts, physical cash, Treasury bills

- Property or land and any structure that is permanently attached to it

- Personal property—everything that you own such as boats, collectibles, household furnishings, jewelry, vehicles

- Investments—annuities, bonds, the cash value of life insurance policies, mutual funds, pensions, retirement plans, (IRA, 401(k), 403(b), etc.) stocks

Your net worth is calculated by subtracting your liabilities from your assets. Essentially, your assets are everything you own, and your liabilities are everything you owe. A positive net worth indicates that your assets are greater in value than your liabilities; a negative net worth signifies that your liabilities exceed your assets.

We all want to increase our assets, because creating more income is the key to being able to compound your overall assets portfolio.

Our goal is to teach you how to increase your B & I quadrants, respectively, since they are the two most tax efficient ones.

The Richest Man in Babylon

The Richest Man in Babylon, written in 1929 by George Samuel Clayson, teaches money basics. While teaching the material to others, I found that a high percentage of people have already heard of these rules yet hadn't had anyone teach them practical ways to use them to grow their assets. The book teaches seven rules.

Rule #1: Start thy purse to fatten. Translation: *Pay yourself first.*

This rule needs no explanation but, for some reason, most people do not follow it. We have been conditioned to pay our expenses first due to the fear instilled in us around losing good credit or something else. That fear should be minimized when you follow rule number two.

By paying yourself first, you can increase your chances of getting to the "I" Quadrant. Here are a few examples of how you might do it.

- **Contribute to your company's 401(k) plan.** If they don't offer one, then set up an IRA and have the contributions deposited automatically every month, so you don't have to think about it. For most employees, this is a great way to save. However, as a business owner, this is one of the least effective ways. We will discuss this in more detail later and explain why.

🐞 **Pay your mortgage.** If you own your house, your mortgage is a way you pay yourself first, because part of your payment pays down the loan amount. This increases both your equity and the appreciation of your house. For employees, this is a great way to save. However, as a business owner, we can show you a more effective and efficient way to manage your house.

Rule #2: Control thy expenditures. Translation: *Control your spending.*

This rule tends to be overlooked. I have found that those in the "B" and "I" quadrants are more diligent in following this rule. If people followed this, they would be better off on a monthly basis. Controlling spending can help people reach the I Quadrant faster. Make a commitment today to start doing this. For employees, getting a handle on spending can positively affect your finances. For business owners, understanding this rule and what expenses are good or bad can lead to effective compounding of assets.

Rule #3: Make thy gold to multiply. Translation: *Earn a fair rate of return.*

When it comes to growing your assets, why hurry? If you rush to grow your assets faster than you should, you may end up taking on more risk and uncertainty than you realize. You can grow your assets without increasing your risks and uncertainty, and I'll show you how later. In short, don't increase your risk unless, of course, you are completely comfortable with losing money. For business owners, we can show you how to structure a plan to accomplish this effectively. For most employees, slow and steady wins the race. Don't fall into the trap many try to lead you into to take on too much risk or move too fast. Follow these rules and you should be fine.

Rule #4: Guard thy treasures from loss. Translation: *Don't lose money.*

Over the years, I have seen people take more risks and lose more money than feels comfortable to them. Yes, I know that 90+ percent of people probably think I am referring to the stock market. I'm not. Losing money comes in all forms and can include taking risks all across the board. Losing money may mean paying too much credit card interest, paying for unused products and services (gym memberships, anyone?), making rash decisions or not researching enough. A dripping faucet is annoying but usually does not receive the attention it should until the problem becomes a water stain or flood. Business owners and employees alike need to heed this rule.

Rule #5: Make thy dwelling a profitable investment. Translation: *Own real estate.*

Although your personal residence is not an asset, according to the definition, and doesn't have a rate of return on equity in the house, it is still valuable to you. I can show you how to enhance this liability into an asset.

Rule #6: Insure a future income. Translation: *Protect your family.*

Many only translate this rule into the need for insurance. But what about designing your assets to generate income you control? Shifting to the I Quadrant, as in the Cashflow Quadrant, allows you to fulfill this rule's intention.

Rule #7: Increase thy ability to earn. Translation: *Increase your ability to earn.*

This rule is an accumulation of some of the previous rules. By designing your assets to increase your ability to earn, you can control the previous rules and minimize the effects of not following the other rules.

I added this next rule since the topic needs to be understood. This rule has seemed unattainable before yet seems increasingly attainable with each election.

Rule #8: Pay thy "fair" share in taxes. Translation: *Reduce your tax liability.*

Taxes tend to be the largest expense line, along with paying salaries, if you are a business owner. They can quickly eat away at your hard-earned ability to increase assets. The next chapter will discuss types of assets.

CHAPTER TWO

Assets and Their Stages

A*n asset is anything of value or a resource of value that can be converted into cash.* The most common conversion of an asset is in the form of income. Let me ask you a couple questions. First question, what does the IRS tax? Correct, income. Second question, what creates income? That's right, assets. Did you know you are an asset? If you generate an income and the IRS says you can be taxed on that income, then you are an asset yourself.

In relation to the *Cashflow Quadrant*, we discussed how negotiation happens between employers, employees, customers, and companies as to what constitutes our value and worth. Income results from those negotiations. For a business, it is the price they charge for a product or service. For an individual, it's their paycheck. The income we generate dictates expenses, or the expenses dictate income. Either way, reciprocity exists between the two. Most people allow their expenses to increase based on their income. Both existing assets and building your assets allow you to generate income without increasing your personal expenses. This connects to the rules in *The Richest Man in Babylon*. Each asset needs to follow those rules. As we build our assets, we are essentially following the *Cashflow Quadrant*. Assets create leverage for your overall plan and that equates to control.

Asset Building

When looking at assets, use ones that will provide flexibility and control in your favor when it comes to the stages of assets. Each asset has its own rules. Understanding those rules allows for you to plan for the associated positive or negative outcomes. No perfect asset exists, but a plan can be created to allow assets to complement each other. For example, think back when you were a kid playing with your favorite toy. You would develop these elaborate stories and scenarios and barely notice the time passing. Now think back when your best friend came over. You played together and used the same toys, and the whole day passed by. Your stories would play off each other by adding other types of toys. Eventually, all the toys were out and part of the overall story. By "buddying up," you can play off each other's strengths and creativity and work together.

This same rule applies when building assets. We call this process the **Asset Buddy Building System**. By "buddying" assets, we allow them to work together in order to enhance the compounding of each other. With multiple assets compounding, you want to reach what Robert Kiyosaki calls the Velocity of Money.[6]

> *The reality is that real investors do not park their money. They move their money. It is a strategy known as the velocity of money. A true investor's money is always moving, acquiring new assets, and then moving on to acquire even more assets. Only amateurs park their money.*

At this stage, the compounding of your assets can out-pace your ability to earn. This is a good point to stop and discuss compounding.[7]

> *Compounding typically refers to the increasing value of an asset due to the interest earned on both a principal and accumulated interest. This phenomenon, which is a direct realization of the time value of money concept, is also known as compound interest. Compound interest works on both assets and liabilities. While compounding boosts the value of an asset more rapidly, it can also increase the amount of money owed on a loan, as interest accumulates on the unpaid principal and previous interest charges.*

If you are already accomplishing this, then the next stage would be to enhance the compounding to out-perform your current situation. That would be your new

Velocity of Money point. As with the game of tag, you get tagged—and are out—the moment you stop and just stand there (park your money).

The Three Asset Stages

Each asset, including yourself, passes through the Beginning, Middle, and Ending.

Stage 1 / Beginning: Contribution. Here, you contribute (invest or buy) a dollar amount. Once this stage happens, the asset enters Stage 2.

Stage 2 / Middle: Accumulation. Assets begin to compound in the Accumulation Stage, which happens differently with each asset. Understanding the rules of assets helps you to know how this can be enhanced with efficiencies equal to the asset. The Accumulation Stage tends to be the longest one, depending on the overall plan and how an asset is used within the plan. Remember, the purpose of an asset is to generate income which can be:

1) deferred to allow the growth and compounding of the assets over a designated time period, or

2) activated now to allow other assets to accomplish number one.

Once income is activated from an asset, it enters Stage 3 which is the Distribution Stage.

Stage 3 / Ending: Distribution. Income is distributed out of the asset to allow other assets to take full advantage of the Accumulation Stage. Remember, each asset has a purpose in an overall plan. And a good plan will take advantage of each stage when it is most efficient for your plan, which is different with each client and their situation.

Each asset and their respective rules respond differently to these stages. When we have a purposeful plan in place, we are proactive instead of reactive. When we have no plan, we are forced to be reactive, and that's not always beneficial to a plan.

Three Great Truths

You have heard of all three. However, the first two have been considered what has been, and will always be, constant. This held true until the third truth entered the picture.

Ready for the first great truth?

Death. We will all die, and we can't change that. Of course, taxes is number two. We will all pay taxes. Later, we'll show you how to move closer to paying only your fair share.

Debt is the third, and it's important to plan for it. Are you going to allow yourself to be affected by the government's debt? Do you have debt? If you do, is it good or bad debt?

If yes, put this book down and go to www.usdebtclock.org

CHAPTER THREE

Economic Termites

You'll see in the beginning of this chapter I will say how "events could cause harm to your plan of building assets." In our opinion, whether you are a business owner now, or through our process you become a business owner due to asset building, no separation exists between your business and personal lives. When decisions are made in one area, they affect the other. As business owners, you can compartmentalize certain aspects of your business and personal lives, yet each affects the other when you look at the big picture. You may have to make business decisions, which affect your personal life and vice versa.

When talking about building assets and financial well-being, you need to review how certain events could cause harm to your asset-building plan. As you build assets, you are essentially in the I Quadrant (Investor) of the Cashflow Quadrant. Depending upon the plan and its execution, building your assets will cause you to enter either the S Quadrant (Self-Employed) and/or the B Quadrant (Business). Again, we're aiming to enhance your B Quadrant and I Quadrant areas.

Take a look at these pictures of how termites can cause damage without you even knowing about it. Notice the exterior is intact but the inside is riddled with holes. When the inside loses its strength the outside façade deteriorates. The strength of your business is the integrity of the inside and not the exterior.

By now, you must be wondering about what these Economic

Termites are. Please note this is not an exhaustive list:

- 🐜 Taxes
- 🐜 Inflation
- 🐜 Time
- 🐜 Laws and Regulations
- 🐜 Debt
- 🐜 Interest Rates
- 🐜 Procrastination

- Running out of Money
- Economic Volatility
- Stress and Sleepless Nights
- Serious Health Event

We address the four major Economic Termites here, and you'll learn why we focus on them later. Keep in mind that focusing on four of them does not mean we do not address all of the Economic Termites in our planning. In fact, by following the rules from *The Richest Man in Babylon*, we inherently plan for the majority of them.

As you read the rest of the book, you'll see how these affect your asset-building plan.

- Taxes
- Inflation
- Time
- Laws and Regulations

Note: Debt is another major economic termite but I have not included an in depth look due to the varying concerns today and the many areas this encompasses. I am working on a separate report to address this economic termite.

Before we go into each of them further, we need to address some essential economic terms.

1) Opportunity Costs

2) Difference between Revenue vs Income vs Life-style Income vs Non-Lifestyle Income

3) Expenses

Opportunity Costs

Opportunity Cost is an economic term that applies to both our business and personal lives.

> *"A benefit, profit, or value of something that must be given up to acquire or achieve something else. Since every resource (land, money, time, etc.) can be put to alternative uses, every action, choice, or decision has an associated opportunity cost. Opportunity costs are fundamental costs in economics and are used in computing cost benefit analysis of a project. Such costs, however, are not recorded in the account books but are recognized in decision making by computing the cash outlays and their resulting profit or loss."*[8]

What does this mean to us? How does this affect your business of asset building? Simply put, we need to be mindful on what or where we spend our energy, money and time. Let's say you decide to go to lunch with a group of old friends to reminisce. Alternately, you could attend a training to learn about new techniques in asset building, which has the potential of helping you reach the next level. If you visit with your friends, how would not attending the training affect your business? In this case, we don't know the opportunity cost. We don't know if you would have ended up learning how a new technique could help you improve your business to hit your goals. We won't know if that training could lead you to an asset to become successful or hit the Velocity of Money moment sooner. As we address each Economic Termite, we'll look at the actual or estimated Opportunity Cost, so we can see the effect in numbers.

Revenue vs Income vs Lifestyle Income vs Non-Lifestyle Income

In business, we want revenue to pay for your expenses, which results in a profit or loss. Generating positive cash flow allows you to have long-term growth. Ideally, we limit taxable income as much as possible within the guidelines laid out by the IRS.

> *Revenue[9] and income aren't the same. When understanding the difference, we need to take a step back and dissect each term and where they should be placed.*

Revenue is the income generated by a business from goods or services, or any other use of capital or assets, associated with the main operations of an organization before any costs or expenses are deducted. Also referred to as earnings or gross profit.

Usually, revenue appears as the top item in an Income (profit and loss) Statement from which all charges, costs, and expenses are subtracted to arrive at Net Income. The Net Income or Profit appears at the bottom. Side note: Each business expense, even though it is an expense, provides tax savings as a business deduction. We'll talk later about two different types of deductions.

When wearing your business owner hat and referencing income, you're usually referring to Revenue. If you are talking about "Net Income," then you may use the terms "income" or "profit/loss." For some non-business owners, this becomes confusing since the term "income" often refers to income to the individual, which is different.

> Income[10] is the flow of cash or cash-equivalents received from work (wages or salary), capital (interest or profit), or land (rent).

For a business, this is an expense line item titled as Salaries and Wages on the Form 1040 personal tax return. For the individual, this is your personal balance sheet topline. If we were to use the example of a personal checking account, your personal expenses are subtracted from this balance in your checking account to create the new balance. You also receive income as an employee of your business, which is an expense to the business just it would be for any other employee.

Profit comes to you as a K1 distribution if you set your business up as a S-Corporation.

I use the term "Lifestyle Income/Expenses" to indicate what your personal income is used for, usually monthly expenses or budget. (In general, I dislike the term "budget," because people view this as a negative term. Most people cannot stick to their budget, and they feel frustrated about it.) By the way, when I refer to budget income, I do not mean you have to eat hot dogs and rice to survive. Lifestyle Income/Expenses should take into account how you want to spend your money. If you spend $500 a month on movies, then that is part of your Lifestyle Income/Expenses. There's no judgment about how or where you spend your money, because it's yours.

Non-Lifestyle Income is that discretionary income *not* used as Lifestyle Income. When we reach the section on taxes, we'll revisit these terms so you can see how there are Opportunity Costs associated with certain Lifestyle Income/Expenses and Non-Lifestyle Income. By understanding these terms—Revenue, Income, Lifestyle Income/Expenses, and Non-Lifestyle Income—you'll know what I mean later and can see how they can be used for or against your benefit.

Positive Cash flow vs Taxable Income

A difference exists between positive cash flow and taxable income. With some assets, you can have positive cash flow but not have taxable income. For example, we can make this distinction of positive cash flow with real estate. Most of the time, when you hear about real estate experts encouraging people to invest in real estate, they use the term positive cash flow. We want to make a distinction between the two terms, because you're a business owner. And, as a business owner, you have to generate income from your business—both as a Salary (W2) and profit (K1). I ask my clients whether they need more income and created a formula to answer the question.

Basic Income Formula

Adjusted Gross Income (AGI) – Lifestyle Income = Non-Lifestyle Income

I use this formula with clients during our Appreciable Deduction Planning process. Let me define the terms and explain the formula, so we can figure out if you need more income or not.

Adjusted Gross Income (AGI) is defined as gross income minus adjustments to income.[11]

That really isn't too helpful, so here's another definition from Turbotax:[12]

The AGI calculation is relatively straightforward.

🐜 *It is equal to the total income you report that's subject to income tax—such as earnings from your job, self-employment, dividends and interest from a bank account—minus specific deductions, or "adjustments" that you're eligible to take.*

🐜 *Your AGI is calculated before you take the standard or itemized deductions—which you report in later sections of the return.*

To use the formula to answer the income question, we do some basic math. Subtract what you spend on a monthly basis and multiply that by 12 months.

From a business perspective, this is the profit and loss statement. As an individual, we do the same thing. We take our revenue (income) and subtract expenses, and the result is profit and loss. Profit is taxable income. If all I need is the income to pay for my expenses, then I'm basically giving the rest away to the IRS as taxable income. Let's say my AGI is $300,000. Let's say my expenses are $200,000. That leaves $100,000, which is a 24% tax bracket as married filing joint. So I'd be paying $24,000 more than I need to be in taxes.

Note: The first three chapters in section 1 gave you a foundation and basic understanding of the terminology we use. The next four chapters dive into the Economic

Termites in more detail. Section 2 shares a story to illustrate the concepts from section 1, so you can learn a way that works best for you. As educators and consultants, we want to help you with the learning process, so you have a good foundation if you decide to proceed with building assets.

CHAPTER FOUR

Termite #1—Taxes

This topic creates a huge debate. When it comes down to it, politics aside, both side of the political aisle will do what they feel is in the best interest of _____ (fill in the blank). Taxes affect your hard work, which equates to revenue and income. Before we continue, let me say that this is not tax advice, and the numbers used are estimated calculations to illustrate the point and affect on you. Additionally, scenarios can quickly become complicated, so I will do my best to simplify the explanation.

To begin, you need to have a basic understanding of what the personal income tax brackets look like and how they function based on the federal tax rates. We will not go into *state* tax brackets, because each state is different. Quite honestly, the state tax brackets make the tax liability look scarier. Before we continue to look at the federal tax brackets, I want to explain what I'm referring to when you see the term "tax liability."

A liability is:[13]

1) *In the finance world, it is a claim against the assets, or legal obligations of a person or organization, arising out of past or current transactions or actions. They require mandatory transfer of assets, or provision of services, at specific dates or in determinable future.*

2) *In the Accounting world, it is accounts and wages payable, accrued rent and taxes, trade debt, and short and long-term loans. Owners' equity is also termed a liability because it is an obligation of the company to its owners.*

After reading the definition above and including the word "tax" before "liability," you can see why I use the term here.

When filing your federal tax returns, you file both a corporate return and personal return. Your personal return is the Form 1040, which is the summary of all your income from your various business entities (corporate returns). Simply put your personal tax return (1040) is your financial statement for the IRS to view how the health of your financial strength and cash flow are performing. You are their asset as is all tax payers. It is all about business and what assets create cash flow and to what level. This is why and how the federal government establishes a budget for spending. We hear about it every year. At the top of your funnel (see Figure 1) is your income from what-ever income sources you have. That income, profit or loss, travels down the income funnel to be summarized on your Form 1040 personal return.

If you own a business (B Quadrant) or are an investor (I Quadrant) and file a corporate tax return or you have various other assets, each of those generates income.

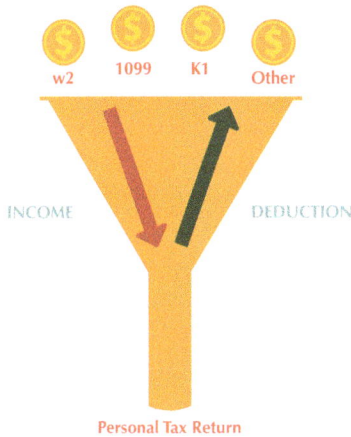

Figure 1

Returning to the federal tax bracket, let us go through how it is structured and set up. In Figure 2, we see an example of "Married Filing Joint," which means you both, as a married couple, are on the tax return jointly.

2018 Federal Tax Brackets
Married Filing Jointly

Taxable income is over	But not over	Plus	Of the amount over	The Tax Owed is	
$0	$19,050	10%	$0	0	0
$19,050	$77,400	12%	19,050	1,905	7,002
$77,400	$165,000	22%	77,400	8,907	19,272
$165,000	$315,000	24%	165,000	28,179	36,000
$315,000	$400,00	32%	315,000	64,179	27,200
$400,000	$600,00	35%	400,000	91,379	70,000
$600,000		37.0%	600,000	161,379	

Figure 2

The bracket is broken down into income ranges, and each bracket has a certain taxable percentage rate (between 10% and 37%). In the first two columns, you can see income ranges that fall into that tax rate range. When your income hits a new bracket, you owe that next higher tax bracket amount.

For any income within that taxable income bracket range, you pay additional taxes based on the percentage of income within that range. So when your income increases from the 10% tax bracket range to the 12% tax bracket range, you will owe $1,905 in taxes. Any income between $19,050 and $77,400 will be taxed at 12%.

Example: Let's say your income is $50,000. The difference between $50,000 and $19,050 is $30,950. The

$30,950 will be taxed at 12%, so the additional taxes will be $3,714 ($30,950 x 12%). When you add the $1,905 from the previous bracket and the $3,714 from the new bracket, your total tax owed is $5,619. (*This example only demonstrates how tax brackets work and are not actual calculations.*)

Can I assume we are on the same page now?

Most of my clients have a lifestyle within the 24-32% tax brackets. Notice I wrote "lifestyle" and not "income." Lifestyle Income is what you use to live on and pay for your house, cars, schools, food, entertainment, etc. Income is what you receive and is often above what we call Lifestyle Income/Expenses.

Avoid the "Tax Bracket Rat Race."

At this point, I'd like to address the need to stay away from the tax bracket rat race, which begins when people are more concerned with how much they make rather than how much they keep. In my practice, we're focused on what you *keep* because what you *earn* is tax expensive. If your income is above your Lifestyle Income/Expenses, it means you're paying taxes on income you don't need to live, and you haven't been given advice on how to *offset* or *Limit* unnecessary taxation. We call the income that exceeds what you need to live "Non-Lifestyle Income."

A Scenario of How We Help Clients Avoid Unnecessary Taxes

Let's say you come to me and say, *"Hey Robert, I have an AGI (Adjusted Gross income) of $500,000. I pay my quarterly taxes, but I still have to write a check to the IRS to pay more taxes when it comes time to file. This is crazy!"*

Remember our basic formula AGI - Lifestyle Income = Non-Lifestyle Income. So when I add dollar amounts, it looks like: $500,000 - $300,000 = $200,000. To see how this formula is affected in the federal tax bracket, look at Figure 3.

2018 Federal Tax Brackets							AGI	Your Tax (before)
Married Filing Jointly							$500,000	$126,379
Taxable income is over	But not over	Plus	Of the amount over		The Tax Owed is			
$0	$19,050	10%	$0	0	to	0	$19,050	$0
$19,050	$77,400	12%	19,050	1,905	to	7,002	$77,400	$8,907
$77,400	$165,000	22%	77,400	8,907	to	19,272	$165,000	$28,179
$165,000	$315,000	24%	165,000	28,179	to	36,000	$315,000	$64,1179
$315,000	$400,00	32%	315,000	64,179	to	27,200	$400,000	$91,379
$400,000	$600,00	35%	400,000	91,379	to	70,000	$100,000	$35,000
$600,000		37.0%	600,000	161,379	to			

Figure 3

Current situation:

The yellow box (with $500,000 in it) shows the AGI. When we chart this to the federal tax bracket, your income falls into the 35% bracket. However, we don't pay tax on the full income at 35%. Since your income maxes out the 32% tax bracket, you will pay $91,379 in tax. The remaining $100,000 of income falls in the 35% tax bracket and gets taxed at 35% or $35,000. When you add the two, you see you have $126,379 in total tax owed.

To continue the explanation of your current situation, look below at Figure 4.

AGI	Your Tax (before)	Lifestyle Income	Your Tax (after)	Non-Lifestyle Income
$500,000	$126,379	$300,000	$60,579	$200,000
$19,050	$0	$19,050	$0	$19,050
$77,400	$8,907	$77,400	$8,907	$77,400
$165,000	$28,179	$165,000	$28,179	$165,000
$315,000	$64,1179	$315,000	$32,400	$115,000
$400,000	$91,379			
$100,000	$35,000			

Figure 4

Here, we add your Lifestyle Income/Expenses to the tax bracket, and you can see how your total tax drops to $60,579. Through the formula, we found that $200,000 of your income is your Non-Lifestyle Income, so your taxable income (Lifestyle Income/Expenses) is the only income taxed. By incorporating this strategy, we find a tax savings of $65,800 by shifting Non-Lifestyle Income back up the Income Funnel to the corporate tax return. And we do this by implementing our Appreciable Deduction Planning process.

We have been conditioned to fear the IRS or even hate them. Sure there may be cause in certain instances based on experiences. But what if we looked at from this perspective. As we read earlier the IRS reviews your tax returns as a financial statement of one of their businesses so as a business owner yourself you have a partner in the IRS.

Not from a negative standpoint but from a positive. You see if you have a partner there is a relationship that both parties bring to the table. In this situation you run the business and they provide you financial support. Now not from the stand point of loaning you money, that is the bank and lenders job. But they do provide financial support by providing tax deductions, tax incentives, tax credits, tax rebates and other incentives to encourage your business to succeed.

Why in the world do I take this view point? First of all the negative is counter productive because you need the IRS. At any point and time they could tax your business on its revenue (topline) income and not the net income. But more importantly, they want to see you succeed because your success leads to hiring tax payers, employees and self employed contractors. You as a B Quadrant are helping grow the E and S quadrants respectively.

You are starting another asset for the IRS, you are starting another revenue stream for their business.

Then move "This process is similar to traveling . . . all the way to . . . to navigate the "route" with efficiency. Above the top page before "A deduction typically includes . . . and ends . . . such as a 401k profit sharing plan.

Non-Appreciable Deduction and Appreciable Deduction

A deduction[14] typically includes "expenses that the taxpayer incurs during the year that can be applied against or subtracted from their gross income in order to figure out how much tax is owed." From a business perspective, we can use the term Expense, which the IRS allows us to deduct from our Revenue.

Revenue – Expenses = Profit or Loss

The IRS doesn't tax expenses or revenue. Expenses are a tax decudction, which equals tax savings. Basically, two types of Deductions exist. The first, Non-Appreciable Deductions, includes those expenses that do not increase in value after you have spent the money, such as office furniture, office supplies, or a company vehicle. The second, Appreciable Deductions, can grow in value over the original value and can include retirement plans, such as a 401K profit sharing plan.

This process is similar to traveling from point A to Point B. If we planned to drive from Los Angeles, CA to Denver, CO, we would look at a map to plan our route. Let's say the map represents the IRS Tax Code. We have choices on the ways we can travel from one city to the other. Since we want the most efficient way, we plug our itinerary into the GPS to guide us. When we encounter a detour, the GPS efficiently directs us around it. When it comes to taxes, you want to find your "tax planning GPS" to navigate the "route" with efficiency.

In the Income Funnel, you can see the right side shows how Deductions can flow back up the Income Funnel to corporate returns as Deductions. The beneficial strategy we use with clients is to shift Non-Lifestyle Income up the Income Funnel as an Appreciable Deduction, which allows you to minimize tax liability. Although we prefer Appreciable Deductions, there are times when it makes sense to use Non-Appreciable Deduction as per the IRS Tax Codes.

Note: Remember my explanation above about finding the right GPS. If you go to the website www.IRS.gov and search deductions, you can get a list of IRS publications and further explanations. I suggest finding the right GPS for your situation.

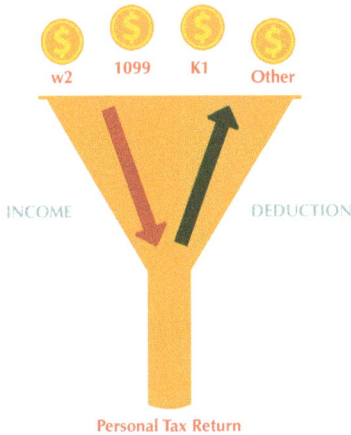

Personal Tax Return

Opportunity Cost

Opportunity Cost enters the picture when we have the possibility of placing this income where it could appreciate and work hard for you. To put numbers to this example, let's look at the Opportunity Cost associated with your current planning. Based on our example on page 39 figure 4, Let's say the IRS receives this $65,800 of taxes on income you have said, according to our formula, you do not need.

In Figure 5, you can see how much that $65,800 appreciates in one year. In Figure 6, we find the Opportunity Cost for the same $65,800 saved every year over a 20-year period. Both examples assume a basic 5% increase over a 20-year period and show the Opportunity Cost of a 5% appreciation value on the $65,800 saved from tax liability. To illustrate the point, we assumed:

- this represents a 45-year-old person wanting to retire at age 65,

- that 20 years of compounding of 5% appreciation will mean that same $65,800 is now valued at $174,587 (one year on the left side),

- that the same $65,800, calculated on an annual basis for 20 years, will be worth $2,175,740 (every year on the right side).

One Year	
Capital Loss	$65,800
True Cost of Capital Loss:	
Age When $$ was lost	45
Retirement Age	65
Years Lost	20
Estimated Growth	5.00%
True Cost of Capital Loss	
$174,587	

Every Year	
Capital Loss	$65,800
True Cost of Capital Loss:	
Age When $$ was lost	45
Retirement Age	65
Years Lost	20
Estimated Growth	5.00%
True Cost of Capital Loss	
$2,175,740	

Figure 5   Figure 6

Above, we showed you the potential Opportunity Cost to common planning models. See why the IRS wants to partner—how may E & S quadrants can you hire? Please keep in mind this is for illustrative purposes only. Below is an illustration of what happens when we implement our Appreciable Deduction Planning process. In the illustration above, we only show the tax liability. Meaning the tax on our extra Non-Lifestyle Income of $200,000 when we show the whole $200,000 moving through our Appreciable Deduction Planning process—see Figures 7 and 8—then we see the power of protecting your unnecessary income (Non-Lifestyle Income) from the Economic Termites of taxes.

One Year	
Capital Loss	$200,000
True Benefit of Capital Restructuring:	
Age When $$ was lost	45
Retirement Age	65
Years Lost	20
Estimated Growth	5.00%
True Benefit	
$530,660	

Every Year	
Capital Loss	$200,000
True Benefit of Capital Restructuring:	
Age When $$ was lost	45
Retirement Age	65
Years Lost	20
Estimated Growth	5.00%
True Benefit	
$6,613,191	

Figure 7   Figure 8

So far, we have illustrated income from a federal tax bracket. If you are in a state with high state income taxes, then you can throw that on top of the scenario. Please note we have not included any of the 3.8% for

Obamacare, so ask your tax professional about this.

Bottom line: The Opportunity Cost associated with tax liability is expensive.

We can do something about that expense. The IRS provides you with guidlines to lower Adjusted Gross Income (AGI) by shifting income you do not currently need for your lifestyle into our Appreciable Deduction Planning process, so it can appreciate year over year.

Businesses receive benefits from tax laws since most of these tax laws are created for you, the business, versus the W2 employee. The IRS *wants* you to save on taxes, and that's why you have the ability to deduct expenses. What the IRS doesn't want is for you to lie, cheat, deceive them, or evade taxes. We are all going to pay taxes, and you want to pay only your "fair" share. We do *not* advocate not paying them. We *do* advocate paying taxes on income you need to live your lifestyle. All other excess income should be put to better use. The IRS *wants* you to use deductions or else they would get rid of all of them. When the IRS limits the use of a deduction, it often means people have abused it.

Through our consulting practice, every proposed plan uses deductions that are for the betterment of your business—to protect your business and provide sustainability. This helps the community since the business provides jobs by hiring employees and provides products and/or services the community uses. When a business grows, it hires more employees and those employees pay income taxes on their W2 income. The IRS likes these additional taxes.

CHAPTER FIVE

Termite #2—Inflation

nflation is a sustained, rapid increase in prices, as measured by some broad index (such as Consumer Price Index) over months or years, and mirrored in the correspondingly decreasing purchasing power of the currency. It has its worst effect on the fixed-wage earners and is a disincentive to save.

There is no one single, universally accepted cause of inflation, and the modern economic theory describes three types of inflation:

1) *Cost-push inflation is due to wage increases that cause businesses to raise prices to cover higher labor costs, which leads to demand for still higher wages.*

2) *Demand-pull inflation results from increasing consumer demand financed by easier availability of credit.*

3) *Monetary inflation caused by the expansion in money supply (due to printing more money by a government to cover its deficits).*

—Business Dictionary:[15]

In other words, inflation is *"described as continuously rising prices, or the continuous fall in value of the dollar."* [16]

For a more detailed explanation of what the Consumer Price Index[17] is and how it works, please go to the Bureau of Labor Statistics website www.bls.gov.

Rule of 72

Before we talk about the history of inflation—exciting, right?—let me make a quick point. When we do our planning, history indicates the future. As a society, we may say we don't learn from history. In our planning methodology, we strive to learn from it.

So the Rule of 72, according to Investopedia, is:[18]

> *. . . a quick, useful formula that is popularly used to estimate the number of years required to double the invested money at a given annual rate of return.*
>
> *While calculators and spreadsheet programs like excel sheets have inbuilt functions to accurately calculate the precise time required to double the invested money, the rule of 72 comes in handy for*

mental calculations to quickly gauge an approximate value.

Alternatively, it can compute the annual rate of compounded return from an investment given how many years it will take to double the investment.

Years required to double investment = 72 / compound annual interest rate

Example: If you think you can get a rate of return of 8% from XYZ investment, then you can plug the numbers into the formula to get an idea of how long it will take your money to double.

$$9 \text{ years} = 72 / 8.0\%$$

You will see how the Rule of 72 can be used when estimating inflation growth as we move through this chapter. Remember our discussion on compounding, though. This can work for you or against you. Inflation is an example of how it can work against you.

History of Inflation

You can see what inflation has been since the year 2000, according to the US Inflation Calculator.

Year	Jan	Feb	Mar	Apr	May	Jun	Jul	Aug	Sep	Oct	Nov	Dec	Ave
2018	2.1	2.2	2.4	2.5	2.8	2.9	2.9	2.7	2.3	2.5	2.2		
2017	2.5	2.7	2.4	2.2	1.9	1.6	1.7	1.9	2.2	2.0	2.2	2.1	2.1
2016	1.4	1.0	0.9	1.1	1.0	1.0	0.8	1.1	1.5	1.6	1.7	2.1	1.3
2015	-0.1	0.0	-0.1	-0.2	0.0	0.1	0.2	0.2	0.0	0.2	0.5	0.7	0.1
2014	1.6	1.1	1.5	2.0	2.1	2.1	2.0	1.7	1.7	1.7	1.3	0.8	1.6
2013	1.6	2.0	1.5	1.1	1.4	1.8	2.0	1.5	1.2	1.0	1.2	1.5	1.5
2012	2.9	2.9	2.7	2.3	1.7	1.7	1.4	1.7	2.0	2.2	1.8	1.7	2.1
2011	1.6	2.1	2.7	3.2	3.6	3.6	3.6	3.8	3.9	3.5	3.4	3.0	3.2
2010	2.6	2.1	2.3	2.2	2.0	1.1	1.2	1.1	1.1	1.2	1.1	1.5	1.6
2009	0	0.2	-0.4	-0.7	-1.3	-1.4	-2.1	-1.5	-1.3	-0.2	1.8	2.7	-0.4
2008	4.3	4.0	4.0	3.9	4.2	5.0	5.6	5.4	4.9	3.7	1.1	0.1	3.8
2007	2.1	2.4	2.8	2.6	2.7	2.7	2.4	2.0	2.8	3.5	4.3	4.1	2.8
2006	4.0	3.6	3.4	3.5	4.2	4.3	4.1	3.8	2.1	1.3	2.0	2.5	3.2
2005	3.0	3.0	3.1	3.5	2.8	2.5	3.2	3.6	4.7	4.3	3.5	3.4	3.4
2004	1.9	1.7	1.7	2.3	3.1	3.3	3.0	2.7	2.5	3.2	3.5	3.3	2.7
2003	2.6	3.0	3.0	2.2	2.1	2.1	2.1	2.2	2.3	2.0	1.8	1.9	2.3
2002	1.1	1.1	1.5	1.6	1.2	1.1	1.5	1.8	1.5	2.0	2.2	2.4	1.6
2001	3.7	3.5	2.9	3.3	3.6	3.2	2.7	2.7	2.6	2.1	1.9	1.6	2.8
2000	2.7	3.2	3.8	3.1	3.2	3.7	3.7	3.4	3.5	3.4	3.4	3.4	3.4

Figure 10

Figure 11 illustrates the effect of inflation on income. If you had $1,000 in year 1 (2000) and calculated the average of 2.17 percent, that $1,000 in 17 years (2016) would now have to be $1,440 to equal the same value or purchasing power. In other words, that same $1,000 would have the same purchasing power as $689.

Year	Monthly Income	Inflation %	Increases	Decreases
1	$1,000	2.17%	$1,022	$978
2	$1,000	2.17%	$1,044	$957
3	$1,000	2.17%	$1,067	$936
4	$1,000	2.17%	$1,090	$916
5	$1,000	2.17%	$1,113	$896
6	$1,000	2.17%	$1,137	$877
7	$1,000	2.17%	$1,162	$858
8	$1,000	2.17%	$1,187	$839
9	$1,000	2.17%	$1,213	$821
10	$1,000	2.17%	$1,239	$802
11	$1,000	2.17%	$1,266	$786
12	$1,000	2.17%	$1,294	$769
13	$1,000	2.17%	$1,322	$752
14	$1,000	2.17%	$1,351	$736
15	$1,000	2.17%	$1,380	$720
16	$1,000	2.17%	$1,410	$704
17	$1,000	2.17%	$1,440	$689

Figure 11

Therefore, when we are looking for Appreciable Deductions, which we'll discuss more in a later chapter, we need to appreciate 2.17 percent to stay ahead of, or even with, inflation. As a result, we consider Inflation[19] an Economic Termite. It will eat away at your business infrastructure by 2.17 percent. Over a 30-year period, inflation averaged 2.65 percent. That means your $1,000 will be worth $447 in 30 years.

Cost of goods have changed over the years as well. Take a look at Figure 13 to glimpse the cost changes over the decades.

	New Home	Wages	New Car	Gallon of Gas	Loaf of Bread	1lb Hamburger
1930	$3,845	$1,970	$600	$0.10	$0.09	$0.12
1940	$3,920	$1,725	$850	$0.11	$0.10	$0.20
1950	$8,450	$3,210	$1,510	$0.18	$0.12	$0.30
1960	$12,700	$5,315	$2,600	$0.25	$0.22	$0.45
1970	$23,450	$9,400	$3,450	$0.36	$0.25	$0.70
1980	$68,700	$19,500	$7,200	$1.19	$0.50	$0.99
1990	$123,000	$28,960	$16,950	$1.34	$0.70	$0.89
2008	$238,880	$40,523	$27,958	$2.05	$2.79	$3.99
2013	$289,500	$44,321	$31,352	$3.80	$1.98	$4.68

Figure 13

Figure 14 shows the cost of goods in 1975 compared to what the projected costs would be in 2015 dollars and includes the actual 2015 costs in the far right column.

Cost of Living in the United States 1975 vs 2015			
Good or Service	1975 Cost	1975 Cost (In 2015 Money)	Cost 2015
New House	$48,000	$209,417	$270,200
Median Income	$12,686	$55,347	$51,759
New Car	$3,800	$16,578	$31,252
Minimum Wage	$2.10 / Hour	$9.16 / Hour	$8.25 / Hour
Public College	$1,819	$7,938	$18,943
Private College	$3,776	$16,475	$42,219
Movie Ticket	$2.03	$8.86	$8.17
Gasoline	$0.59 / Gallon	$2.57 / Gallon	$2.38 / Gallon
Postage Stamp	$0.13	$0.57	$0.49
Sugar	$0.65 / 5 Pounds	$2.84 / 5 Pounds	$3.25 / 5 Pounds
Milk	$1.65 / Gallon	$7.20 / Gallon	$3.49 / Gallon
Coffee	$1.12 / Pound	$4.89 / Pound	$4.91 / Pound
Eggs	$0.84 / Dozen	$3.66 / Dozen	$2.08 / Dozen
Bread	$0.28 / Pound	$1.22 / Pound	$1.43 / Pound

Figure 14

Please keep in mind Inflation can vary from state to state or even county to county. This chart uses national averages.

Figure 15 shows how inflation can affect our future.

- 🐜 The blue line assumes all stays the same (no inflation at all),

- 🐜 the dotted orange line represents living expenses increasing due to inflation,

- 🐜 the red line represents the erosion of income due to inflation, and

- 🐜 the green line represents income increasing or staying ahead of inflation.

Which do you prefer? Of course, everyone says the green line. But, too often, we are so busy with our day-to-day lives that it's difficult to visualize how inflation could negatively affect our future. Our planning processes take this Economic Termite into consideration.

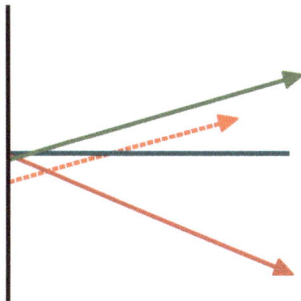

Figure 15

CHAPTER SIX

Termite #3—Time

Time is the indefinite [continuation] of existence and events that occur in apparently irreversible succession from the past through the present to the future.[20]

—Edward Young

Time is a commodity that has to be used with care. Once it has passed, it cannot be found, repeated, or returned. In a lot of cases, time is procrastination. Edward Young refers to procrastination as a "thief of time," Noah St. John of the Huffington Post[21] supports this idea:

1. *Time never stops, never slows down, is always moving.*

2. *Once it's gone, it's gone forever.*

3. *Therefore, time is the one resource that can never be replaced.*

What does the power of time look like?

To see the effect of time, we can observe the effects of doubling a penny every day for 30 days in the following analogy[22] (Figure 16). If you doubled a penny every day for 30 days, your penny would be worth $5,368,709.12 in 30 days. This doesn't take into account any Economic Termites, such as Taxes, Inflation, Time, or Laws/Regulations. The only Economic Termite that could affect our results in a 30-day time period would be Taxes and/or Laws/Regulations. For our illustration, let's just look at Taxes (Figure 17).

Day	Dollars
1	$0.01
2	$0.02
3	$0.04
4	$0.08
5	$0.16
6	$0.32
7	$0.64
8	$1.28
9	$2.56
10	$5.12
11	$10.24
12	$20.48
13	$40.96
14	$81.92
15	$163.84
16	$327.68
17	$655.36
18	$1,310.72
19	$2,621.44
20	$5,242.88
21	$10,485.76
22	$20,971.52
23	$41,943.04
24	$83,886.08
25	$167,772.16
26	$355,544.32
27	$671,088.64
28	$1,342,177.28
29	$2,684,354.56
30	$5,368,709.12

Figure 16

Day	Dollars	Gain	Tax (30%)	Net
1	$0.01	$0.00	$0.00	$0.01
2	$0.01	$0.01	$0.00	$0.02
3	$0.02	$0.02	$0.01	$0.03
4	$0.03	$0.03	$0.01	$0.05
5	$0.05	$0.05	$0.01	$0.08
6	$0.08	$0.08	$0.03	$0.14
7	$0.14	$0.14	$0.04	$0.24
8	$0.24	$0.24	$0.07	$0.41
9	$0.41	$0.41	$0.12	$0.70
10	$0.70	$0.70	$0.21	$1.19
11	$1.19	$1.19	$0.36	$2.02
12	$2.02	$2.02	$0.60	$3.43
13	$3.43	$3.43	$1.03	$5.83
14	$5.83	$5.83	$1.75	$9.90
15	$9.90	$9.90	$2.97	$16.84
16	$16.84	$16.84	$5.05	$28.62
17	$28.62	$28.62	$8.59	$48.66
18	$48.66	$48.66	$14.60	$82.72
19	$82.72	$82.72	$24.82	$140.63
20	$140.63	$140.63	$42.19	$239.07
21	$239.07	$239.07	$71.72	$406.42
22	$406.42	$406.42	$121.93	$690.92
23	$690.92	$690.92	$207.28	$1,174.56
24	$1,174.56	$1,174.56	$352.37	$1,996.76
25	$1,996.76	$1,996.76	$599.03	$3,394.49
26	$3,394.49	$3,394.49	$1,018.35	$5,770.63
27	$5,770.63	$5,770.63	$1,731.19	$9,819.07
28	$9,819.07	$9,819.07	$2,943.02	$16,677.11
29	$16,677.11	$16,677.11	$5,003.13	$28,351.09
30	$28,351.09	$28,351.09	$8,505.33	$48,196.86

Figure 17

The second way to illustrate procrastination is through the analogy of saving early (Figure 18). Let us assume we have person A and person B. Both will save $2,000 a year. However, person B decides to wait to save, so he can travel. After eight years of traveling, he decides it's time to save.

Both people saved $16,000 over an eight-year period. But, since person B waited, the amount that appreciated over the 30 years was different due to time. Some would say that $18,957 isn't that much of a difference. The point isn't this example's particular difference, which could vary from person to person. It's that Economic Termites are destroyers and need to be understood and planned for. Your Opportunity Costs are exponentially affected when combining the Economic Termite of Time with the other Economic Termites of Taxes and Inflation.

Year	A	Balance		B	Balance
1	$2,000	$2,100		$0	$0
2	$2,000	$4,305		$0	$0
3	$2,000	$6,620		$0	$0
4	$2,000	$9,051		$0	$0
5	$2,000	$11.604		$0	$0
6	$2,000	$14,284		$0	$0
7	$2,000	$17,098		$0	$0
8	$2,000	$20,053		$0	$0
9	$0	$21,056		$2,000	$2,100
10	$0	$22,109		$2,000	$4,305
11	$0	$23,214		$2,000	$6,620
12	$0	$24,375		$2,000	$9,051
13	$0	$25,593		$2,000	$11.604
14	$0	$26,873		$2,000	$14,284
15	$0	$28,217		$2,000	$17,098
16	$0	$29,628		$2,000	$20,053
17	$0	$31,109		$0	$21,056
18	$0	$32,664		$0	$22,109
19	$0	$34,298		$0	$23,214
20	$0	$36,013		$0	$24,375
21	$0	$37,813		$0	$25,593
22	$0	$39,704		$0	$26,873
23	$0	$41,689		$0	$28,217
24	$0	$43,773		$0	$29,628
25	$0	$45,962		$0	$31,109
26	$0	$48,260		$0	$32,664
27	$0	$50,673		$0	$34,298
28	$0	$53,207		$0	$36,013
29	$0	$55,867		$0	$37,813
30	$0	$58,661		$0	$39,704
	$16,000			$16,000	

Figure 18

CHAPTER SEVEN

Termite #4—Laws and Regulations

This chapter could become a library of books unto itself, and I could spend pages upon pages on the associated craziness. Instead, I'll show you examples of how certain laws and regulations can be Economic Termites, which affect your business, and the possible Opportunity Costs associated with those Termites. Some Laws and Regulations do benefit us, and I'll highlight a few.

Regulation, according to the website Business Dictionary,[23] has two meanings:

- *General definition: Principal or rule employed in controlling, directing, or managing an activity, organization, or system.*

- *Law definition: Rule based on, and meant to carry out, a specific piece of legislation. Regulations are enforced usually by a regulatory agency formed or mandated to carry out the purpose or provisions of a legislation.*

Before we become serious, I want to point out a few regulations that will make you scratch your head. This Business Insider[24] article, written by Michael Snyder, points out regulations so funny that you just have to laugh. The Federal Registry is the main source to track the various regulations. To give you an idea of how out of control it has gotten, back "in 1936, the number of pages in the Federal Register was about 2,600. Today, the Federal Register is over 80,000 pages long."

1) The city of Philadelphia now requires all bloggers to purchase a $300 business privilege license.

2) The state of Louisiana says that monks must be fully licensed as a funeral directors and actually convert their monasteries into a licensed funeral homes before they will be allowed to sell their handmade wooden caskets.

3) In the state of Massachusetts, all children in daycare centers are mandated by state law to brush their teeth after lunch. In fact, the state even provides the fluoride toothpaste for the children.

4) If you attempt to give a tour of our nation's capital without a license, you could be put in prison for 90 days.

Overall, keep in mind that Laws/Regulations change and there are Opportunity Costs associated with those changes. I will try my best not to insert my own opinion as to whether the Laws/Regulations have validity or not. Although my example refers to politics, I'm not taking a side. In my opinion, when all is said and done, the government compromises all politicians—no matter the political party.

That said, Obamacare caused significant changes. Many heard that taxes would not be increased to pay for this change, yet 20 changes took place, according to Americans for Tax Reform.[25]

- **Obamacare Individual Mandate Excise Tax** (took effect in Jan 2014)

- **Obamacare Employer Mandate Tax** (took effect Jan. 2014)

- **Obamacare Surtax on Investment Income** (Tax hike of $123 billion/took effect Jan. 2013)

- **Obamacare Excise Tax on Comprehensive Health Insurance Plans** (Tax hike of $32 bil/ took effect Jan. 2018)

- **Obamacare Hike in Medicare Payroll Tax** (Tax hike of $86.8 bil/took effect Jan. 2013)

- **Obamacare Medicine Cabinet Tax** (Tax hike of $5 bil/took effect Jan. 2011)

🐜 **Obamacare HSA Withdrawal Tax Hike** (Tax hike of $1.4 bil/took effect Jan. 2011)

🐜 **Obamacare Flexible Spending Account Cap – aka "Special Needs Kids Tax"** (Tax hike of $13 bil/took effect Jan. 2013)

🐜 **Obamacare Tax on Medical Device Manufacturers** (Tax hike of $20 bil/took effect Jan. 2013)

🐜 **Obamacare "Haircut" for Medical Itemized Deduction from 7.5% to 10% of AGI** (Tax hike of $15.2 bil/took effect Jan. 2013)

🐜 **Obamacare Tax on Indoor Tanning Services** (Tax hike of $2.7 billion/took effect July 2010)

🐜 **Obamacare elimination of tax deduction for employer-provided retirement Rx drug coverage in coordination with Medicare Part D** (Tax hike of $4.5 bil/took effect Jan. 2013)

🐜 **Obamacare Blue Cross/Blue Shield Tax Hike** (Tax hike of $0.4 bil/took effect Jan. 1 2010)

🐜 **Obamacare Excise Tax on Charitable Hospitals** (Min$/took effect immediately)

🐜 **Obamacare Tax on Innovator Drug Companies** (Tax hike of $22.2 bil/took effect Jan. 2010)

🐜 **Obamacare Tax on Health Insurers** (Tax hike of $60.1 bil/took effect Jan. 2014)

🐜 **Obamacare $500,000 Annual Executive Compensation Limit for Health Insurance Executives** (Tax hike of $0.6 bil/took effect Jan 2013)

🐜 **Obamacare Employer Reporting of Insurance on W-2** ($min/took effect Jan. 2012)

🐜 **Obamacare "Black liquor" tax hike** (Tax hike of $23.6 billion/took effect immediately)

🐜 **Obamacare Codification of the "economic substance doctrine"** (Tax hike of $4.5 billion/took effect immediately)

The bottom line is that the law caused changes to our personal and business economics. Your profit increases or decreases based on your costs. The cost for my family of five increased from $1,100 to $1,400 a month from 2017 to 2018. That's a 20%+ increase. That increase is the Opportunity Cost that can be shifted from my savings account to insurance. If my premiums stay the same for the next five years, then ***the Opportunity Cost would be $19,892.***

In 2017, a tax change was proposed. According to the *LA Times*, one of the areas discussed was removing the tax deductibility of 401(k) plans.[26] Back in 2014, according to CNBC,[27] President Obama considered removing some of the benefits of 401(k) plans.

"Under Obama's budget plan, higher-income earners would be limited to a tax deduction at the 28 percent level,

even if their current income-tax bracket is much higher.

If this budget actually becomes law, a person who is at the highest marginal tax bracket of 39.6 percent (this doesn't include state income taxes or the 3.8 percent Obamacare tax) would only be entitled to a tax deduction equal to those individuals in the 28 percent tax bracket."

Although this did not happen, some people are still for it. According to Investment Company Institute,[28] "as of December 31, 2017 401(k), plans held an estimated $5.3 trillion in assets and represented 19 percent of the $27.9 trillion in US retirement assets." What would happen if Congress decided to have a special income tax on retirement assets when they are distributed as income? What if they decided all income from an approved retirement account would receive an excise tax of 5% in addition to federal tax brackets?

What could you and I do? Let's look at this math.

Retirement Assets	$27,900,000,000,000
Excise Tax	5.00%
Additional Tax	$1,395,000,000,000

Could the federal government use this extra tax revenue? Do you think the states would also jump on this bandwagon and create their own retirement tax too? Go to the website www.usdebtclock.org. Look at the national debt and the revenue.

SECTION TWO

A Financial Story
of Two Brothers

As I mentioned in the beginning of the book, I read hundreds of books and especially enjoyed the ones more technical in nature. Other times, I liked books that told a story to convey the message, which is what this section of my book does. If you already read section one, you'll probably feel that I'm repeating myself here. And I am. However, I encourage you to read through this part anyway and allow the information to sink in a second time.

One day, two brothers were catching up over dinner. About two years passed since Sam and Jim had had time for conversation beyond small talk, because they'd been busy with life, family and work.

Sam was having a hard time getting ahead. When he complained to Jim via email one day, Jim suggested they meet up in person at their favorite restaurant.

"I'll treat," Jim emailed.

Sam jumped at the offer. In the past, Jim never paid for anything. Sam didn't want to pass up on the opportunity of both a free meal and time with his brother.

At the restaurant, Sam spotted Jim sitting in the back and joined him at the table. Jim smiled widely when Sam appeared. They hugged. Sam noticed something was different about Jim, and he hoped to learn more.

They ordered their meal and a couple of drinks.

"So Sam tell me what is going on. Your last few emails concerned me. Your tone and energy really seemed low."

"Jim, I'm not sure where to start."

"Where do you feel is the start?"

"I feel like I can't get traction. We have a successful business, yet it seems every year we fall farther behind. We have been able to save money in our company 401k and have been able to buy a few rental properties."

Jim nodded and sipped his drink. The ice clinked in the glass as he set it on the table.

"We have been working with a financial advisor, but it just seems like we get the same standard information. We asked our CPA for help and, again, we don't get the advice we need to change things. So each year, we owe more in taxes than the year before."

"That's hard," Jim said.

"I'm just not sure how much longer I can work this hard and have the same results."

Jim listened intently. "I know how you feel, Sam."

"You do?" Sam asked.

"A few years ago we had the same frustration. We found a consulting firm that educated us on what they call "Asset Building." You see, they taught us that each asset has rules and, if we know what the rules are, then we can make educated financial decisions."

Sam took a bite of his steak and kept listening.

"They taught us the basics, which I initially thought was a waste of time. But as we went through their education, we found it was important because everything ties together. They taught us to look at things from the IRS's view point and to understand what they have provided as guidelines."

Sam said, "Jim, what are you talking about!"

"Ok, Sam, we should begin at the beginning."

Jim set his fork down and pulled a notebook out of his pocket. He ripped out some pieces of paper.

"Sam, the key to everything is cash flow. That means understanding how cash flows and the consequences of the flow of cash. Will it be taxable or tax free?"

"Wait a second Jim! Are you telling me there is a way to get tax-free cash?! This doesn't seem to be honest. Jim what have you gotten yourself into?"

Jim laughed loudly.

"Sam, I said the EXACT same thing! Let me continue, and it will all be clear. Trust me. You know who Robert Kiyosaki is? The author of *Rich Dad Poor Dad?*"

Sam nodded and said, "I read it years ago. I really like the way he explained the difference between both dads."

"Yes, exactly. He wrote another book called *Cashflow Quadrant*. He explains the difference between the various ways to earn income."

Jim sketched it out on the paper, and Sam leaned closer to take a look.

Jim explained what the *Cashflow Quadrant* was and where they fell in this quadrant. (Dear Reader: If you want a refresher, please reread the *Cashflow Quadrant* section in chapter one.)

"You see, you and I, as business owners, are in the B Quadrant. Since you own a couple of rental properties, you are also in the I Quadrant (investor). What I found out, though, was that I wasn't thinking like a B or I Quadrant. I had been thinking like an E Quadrant or an employee," Jim said.

Jim explained how it was necessary to increase assets and use the businesses, along with the tax incentives we get as business owners, to enhance our Asset Building.

"Since creating more income is the key to being able to compound your overall assets portfolio, we all want to increase our assets. The firm I work with has one goal: to increase my cash flow. They taught me how to increase our B & I quadrants, since those quadrants are the two most tax efficient. Plus, the IRS wants us to do that, which is why they created them to be more tax efficient in the first place."

"That makes sense. Tell me more about making my business more tax efficient," Sam said.

"No, it isn't about making your business more tax efficient. It already is."

"Oh," Sam said. He took a drink.

"Yeah," Jim said, "It's about understanding the rules of your assets and making *them* more efficient—not just tax wise but while compounding. Besides you, your business is the greatest asset you have."

Jim added that Sam should follow certain rules when it comes to assets and financial well-being.

"A book called *Richest Man in Babylon* describes seven rules that each asset should incorporate. This book offers a simple message and the simplest idea often has the biggest impact."

"True. So what are the rules?"

"I'll tell you. **Rule one is pay yourself first**. This rule needs no explanation, but I didn't pay attention to it for some reason. I had been conditioned to pay my expenses first due to the fear instilled in me over losing this or that. You remember when you first started your business? We focused on survival. Since there wasn't extra revenue to save, the expenses were the first to be paid. But now that we have passed that stage, following this rule is vital."

"I remember that about expenses," Sam said.

"And do you remember I said before that I was still in the E Quadrant and thinking like an employee? This is an example. Paying yourself first is the way you can increase your chances of getting into the I Quadrant," Jim said.

"What are examples of paying yourself first? Are you talking about putting money aside each month in my bank savings account?"

"Good question. As an employee, you contribute to your company's 401(k) plan, through your mortgage payments, to your house. I did this, and you said you did the same thing. As I learned more, I found these both are not efficient. Not to get ahead of myself, let's just say you and I, as *business owners*, can save in better ways for ourselves first."

Sam was intrigued. He wrote down a note to ask about this later.

Jim continued, "**The second rule is to control your spending**. Even though I own my own business, I was less diligent in this rule than I thought I was. I found that I was taking more income from my business than I needed and was causing my tax bill to be too high. From the consultants, I learned I should look at my taxes as an expense like all my other expenses. I reviewed all of my expenses and found I was spending more money than I needed to in order to write them off as tax deductions to save on taxes—not realizing I was throwing money away."

Sam replied, "You know I find it funny you say that, because I do the same thing with my spending. When I talk to my CPA—which isn't much—I hear I need more deductions. So I spend more to get them."

Jim laughed. "I did the same exact thing. That's why I'm walking you through these rules. This is your money. Wouldn't you want to keep it rather than give it away?'"

"Of course!" Sam said. "You know, Jim, we get trained somehow to do things with really no thought to it. Kind of makes me mad."

The waitress came by and told the brothers that she was going on break and introduced them to her replacement. They ordered dessert.

Sam finished his drink, and Jim started talking again.

"**The third rule, earn a fair rate of return,** was something I wasn't focused on. Every time I talked with my financial advisor, he would always focus on rate of return and how we should shift investments to do this and that, but I found I wasn't earning any more."

The waiter set two pieces of pie on the table and left.

"In fact, I felt I was losing money," Jim said, slicing into his pie. "In 2008, when the market took that big drop, I lost a *lot* of money. That took my sights off rule number one. At that point, the last thing I wanted to do was put more money into that rabbit hole."

Sam ate a piece of pie and took notes.

"This rule is related to the old story about the tortoise and the hare. Why was I in such a hurry when it came to growing assets? Growing my assets faster than I should, depending on the asset, meant I was taking on more risk and uncertainty than I may have realized."

"I get it," Sam said.

"You see, if we developed a plan to save on taxes, then that was my rate of return. I was in the 37% tax bracket. By implementing certain strategies using the IRS code, I could lower my income to the 32% tax bracket. More importantly, the money saved was like a 37% or 35% rate of return. If I didn't save that money, it would go to the IRS. With that savings, I was able to hire a new salesperson who has paid for herself and then some."

"Wow," said Sam. "That's impressive."

"I know! Let me have some more of this pie." Jim took a bite before continuing.

"It's good," Sam said. "Just like Grandma's!"

"It is! So I learned we can grow assets without increasing risks and uncertainty. In fact, don't increase your risk. By taking on more risk, people fall into the trap of the next rule."

Sam felt surprised, because he hadn't had anyone look at what it meant to earn a rate of return. He said, "You know, Jim, we see and hear so much about the stock market on TV that you just subconsciously think about stock investing."

"I know," Jim said.

"That makes sense that I should treat saving on taxes as a rate of return. So what is rule four then?"

"**Rule number four is don't lose money.** This rule seemed to be the most commonsense, but I realized we had leaky faucets everywhere in both personal and business finances. The amount of money lost was crazy. Losing money comes in all forms."

"That makes sense," Sam said.

"So we looked at whether we were paying too much in credit card interest, for products and services that I don't use (gym memberships) or making rash decisions without enough research. A dripping faucet is annoying but usually does not receive the attention it deserves until the problem gets out of hand."

"Are you kidding me?" Sam said. "This stuff is so basic and common sense, but I know I haven't thought about it. I know the other business owners I meet with regularly haven't either. We all complain about the same stuff. But we don't talk about this. I guess when you look at $30 here and $50 there, it doesn't look like much until you add it all up."

Jim smiled. "I know. We sat down and added up all the little things and found we were spending money like crazy and didn't even know it. Did we really need Hulu, Netflix, and Amazon Prime accounts plus our normal cable costs? That alone was over $300 a month."

"Yeah," Sam said. "It all adds up."

Jim chimed in, "But here's the crazy thing—that $300 where does it come from?

Sam answered, "from my checking account."

"That's right. Now how did that money get into your checking account?" Jim asked.

Sam answered knowing he was about to have an aha moment, "my paycheck."

Jim asked another question with a big smile knowing he has led Sam down a path he is going to realize the outcome pretty fast, "and what happens to that money?"

Sam initially had a confused look on his face then his face change immediately with the realization what has been happening.

Jim added, "it's taxed as income then it goes into your checking account so if it's $300 then that means it really is $461 taxed at your federal tax bracket of 35% to net $300 out the door."

Sam was dumfounded, you are right! Hat a way to look at it, so that means all my personal expenses need to be looked at from that perspective."

Jim simply nodded his head.

"**Rule number five is to own real estate**. Well, it actually says to make your house a profitable investment. But Robert Kiyosaki wrote that your house is not an investment. An investment is something that generates income for you, and your house doesn't do that."

Sam had finished his pie and sat back in his chair to hear more.

"As you go through this process, you'll see how to use your house as an investment. In fact, what we did improved our tax savings, too. And I should tell you the term 'investment' is rarely used. Instead, we use 'asset,' because you increase your cash flow when you increase your assets. You have to take the opportunity to shift your valuable house into a profitable asset."

"I'm looking forward to hearing more about that," said Sam.

"**Rule number six is to protect your family**. I have to be honest that this took me some time to understand. This rule, like the rule about not losing money, can go different ways. I translated this rule into the need for insurance. Yes, that is important. But what about the basic fact of designing your assets to generate income you can control?"

"I don't know," Sam said.

Jim took a big drink of water. "Remember the *Cashflow Quadrant*. Shifting to the I Quadrant is important. By doing this, I fulfilled this rule's intention."

"And I guess I did that by buying rental properties," Sam said.

"Right," Jim said. "**Rule number seven is increase your ability to earn**. This rule is an accumulation of some of the previous rules. <u>By designing my assets to increase my ability to earn, I can control the previous rules and minimize the effects of not following those rules</u>. By designing an asset-building plan, all the previous rules automatically put this rule into gear. Almost like auto pilot."

Sam said, "I can see that. I see these rules are important, because they keep things simple. The commonsense and practicality in these rules is perfect for what the majority of us want to accomplish."

"That is what I thought, too. **The eighth rule, to reduce tax liability, isn't in the book**. But you'll see it should be. When reviewing all the previous rules, you encompass all previous seven rules by adding this one rule."

Sam looked at his watch. They had been talking for two

hours. "Wow. Time flies! I have to get home, but I want to meet again to find out if I can be helped."

Jim replied, "Oh, you can be helped. In fact, you'll find that your business will have purpose and improve once you go through the process. Well, it was great spending this time together. When did you want to meet up again?"

Sam responded, "The sooner the better. How about I swing by your office in a couple days and we can go out for lunch?"

Jim replied, "It probably makes more sense for us to meet with Kevin, who has been helping me with everything I shared with you. How about I give him a call and schedule time for us to meet him in a couple of days?"

"Great, shoot me over the details in a text. Thanks, Jim."

A few days later.

As Sam pulled up to Kevin's office, he saw Jim's car in the parking lot. Sam felt a little nervous—almost like going on a first date—as he walked into the office. He thought that was weird but realized that this conversation could change his life and the lives of his family, employees, and other business associates.

Jim and Kevin stood up to greet Sam when the receptionist led him into Kevin's office.

Jim said, "Sam we were just finishing up a review of

our stuff. Sam, this is Kevin. Kevin, this is my favorite brother, Sam."

"I'm his only brother. Nice to meet you, Kevin."

Kevin smiled. "Nice to meet you, Sam. Jim has shared a lot about you, your business, and your family. Sounds like you have a great family. I look forward to meeting them soon. So I understand you guys had an enlightening conversation over dinner a few days ago."

"Yes. We talked about the *Cashflow Quadrant* and *The Richest Man in Babylon* books. The simplicity and power of the messages impressed me."

"Those books influenced me a lot," Kevin said.

"Jim said you were going to show me your process today," Sam said.

Kevin replied, "Well, we'll see. We still have some educating to do. Through that education process, you'll get a glimpse of some of our process. If you are okay with it, let's jump right in. Oh, before we start, did you want some water or coffee?"

"No, I'm good. Let's get started. I am a bit nervous."

Kevin laughed and said, "That happens. You are about to experience a mind shift. This is hard for some and the timing is perfect for others. I see you as the latter."

"We'll see," said Sam smiling.

Kevin started, "Since you guys already talked about *Cashflow Quadrant* and *The Richest Man in Babylon*, we are going to talk about the **three stages of an asset**. Before we review those, I need to define some terms, so we are all on the same page.

"We'll start with the **definition of an asset**. An asset is anything that generates revenue or income. Can we agree that the most common result of an asset is in the form of income?"

Jim and Sam both nodded.

"For example, you are an asset. Since you work for yourself, you generate an income. And you are an asset if the IRS says you can be taxed on the income you generate."

"Okay," said Sam.

"The tricky thing about income, though, is most people don't follow rule number two. They allow their expenses to increase based on their income. Let me take a step back for a second. Once we have income, it tends to dictate our expenses, or the expenses dictate the income. Either way, there is reciprocity between the two. So let me tell you a story of a horse named Income. Income was raised to pull a cart named Expenses. This cart was large, but Income was not so big at the time. At first, Farmer Jim only put enough stuff into the cart so as not to make it too heavy for Income to pull. As Income grew, the cart became easier to pull, so Farmer Jim could put more stuff into the cart. Income stopped growing and, at the same time, grew used to pulling Expenses. Farmer Jim became accustomed to adding stuff into the cart to the point that Income was no longer able to pull Expenses. One day, Farmer Jim headed into town with Income. All of sudden, the cart hit a bump in the road, and Income couldn't pull Expenses any longer."

Jim smiled and Sam nodded.

"Stuck with this realization," Kevin continued, "Farmer Jim didn't know what to do. Sitting on the side of the road, he saw another farmer with two horses pulling a cart the same size as his. Farmer Jim had an idea to buy a second horse, so he walked to the nearest town and purchased a new horse he called Second Income. After hooking up Second Income, Farmer Jim was on his way again."

Kevin sat forward in his chair. Clearly, he was excited to tell this story.

"A few days later, Farmer Jim was heading back to his farm. He had purchased more items, because he had Second Income. With the additional items in his cart, he found his journey home somewhat tedious. As he approached the section of road where he'd become stuck, he worried he would have another problem.

He looked back in his cart, Expenses, and noticed he couldn't find anything to remove. Since he had two horses (Incomes), he figured it would be okay and continued on. But the cart became stuck again. He was in luck, though, because the farmer he saw when he was stuck the first time was nearby. The farmer asked Farmer Jim if he needed any help."

Jim and Sam nodded.

"Farmer Jim graciously accepted the help. The farmer began to push his cart. With his two horses, Income and Second Income, the cart began to move. A happy Farmer Jim asked if there was anything his new friend wanted from the cart. His new friend declined and began walking back to his own farm. Farmer Jim called out to ask his name. 'My name is Asset,' he said."

"Farmer Jim realized that his horses pulled his cart, but his new friend Asset provided the additional advantage. So your income doesn't matter if you aren't following the rules of *The Richest Man in Babylon* and you are not in control of your expenses, because more income doesn't help. Both existing assets and building your assets allow you to generate income without increasing your personal expenses. This connects to the rules in *The Richest Man in Babylon*. Each asset needs to follow those rules, or you'll always be stuck in bumps in the road. As we build our assets, we are essentially following the *Cashflow Quadrant*. Assets create leverage for your overall plan and that equates to control. Does all that makes sense Sam?"

"Wow! Yes, totally. As you were telling the story of Income, I thought about what Jim and I were talking about last week about rule number two. Although my expenses were not necessarily out of control, I found myself spending money to try and save on taxes," replied Sam.

Kevin said, "You'd be surprised how many people do the same thing. So let's discuss Asset Building. When looking at assets, the key is to look at those assets that will provide flexibility and control in your favor when it comes to their phases. We also look at how to handle Economic Termites, which we'll discuss later."

"Got it," Sam said.

"Each asset has its own rules. Understanding those rules allows for you to plan for positive or negative outcomes. Although no perfect asset exists, you can form a plan designed to allow assets to complement each other. For example, think back when you were a kid playing with your favorite toy. You could probably play all day and barely notice the time go by. Now think back when Jim and you both played *together*. Not only were the same toys played with but the time didn't just pass. The entire day passed quickly."

"Yeah," Sam said. He and Jim looked at each other and smiled.

"Now, why was that? When buddying up, you are able to play off each other, and you're able to work together. The same rule goes for building assets. We call this process 'Asset Buddy Building.' Assets buddied together can work together to allow their strengths to enhance the compounding of each other. With multiple assets compounding, you want to reach what Robert Kiyosaki calls the 'Velocity of Money.'"

"I like how that sounds," Sam said.

"I do, too. It describes when the compounding of your assets outearn your ability to earn. If you are already accomplishing this, the next stage is to enhance the compounding so your new point of Velocity of Money outperforms what you are currently doing.

"The three stages are what each asset goes through, including yourself."

Kevin wrote out the stages:

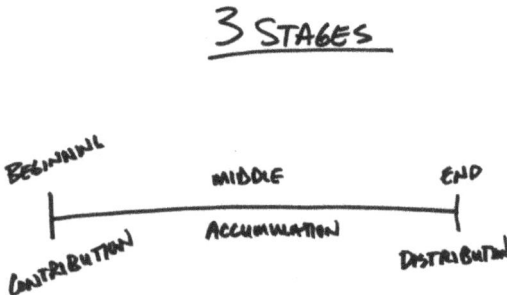

3 STAGES

BEGINNING   MIDDLE   END

CONTRIBUTION   ACCUMULATION   DISTRIBUTION

"Each asset has a beginning. Usually, we use the term "contribution." Here, you Contribute (invest) a dollar amount. This action starts the Stage 1 Contribution Stage. Once the Contribution Stage happens, the asset enters Stage 2, which is the Accumulation Stage. In the Accumulation Stage, assets begin to compound, which is different with each asset. Understanding the rules of assets helps us to know how this can be enhanced with efficiencies equal to the asset."

"Ah, okay," Sam said.

"The Accumulation Stage tends to be the longest, depending on the overall plan and how an asset is being used within the plan. But, remember, the purpose of an asset is to generate income, which can be:

1) deferred to allow the growth and compounding of the assets over a designated time period, or

2) activate the income now to allow other assets to accomplish number one."

Sam nodded.

"Once income is activated from an asset, it enters the Distribution Stage. In this stage, income distributes out of the asset to allow other assets to take full advantage of the Accumulation Stage. Each asset has a purpose in an overall plan, and a good plan allows you to be able to take advantage of each stage when it is most efficient for your plan, which is different with each client and their situation. Does that make sense?"

"Yes," Sam said. He was taking notes.

"Each asset, and their respective rules, respond differently in these three stages. We have been talking about rules of assets, so let's discuss how assets respond or react. When we have a purposeful plan in place, they *respond*. When something *reacts*, that means it was *expecting* an event to occur. When something *responds* then that means it was *not* expecting an event to occur. Does that make sense Sam?"

"Sure does," replied Sam.

"What are those events that assets and their rules respond to?" asked Kevin.

Sam smiled. "I was hoping you'd tell me."

Kevin laughed and said, "Yes. There are three great truths. You have heard of all three. The first two have been considered what has been and will always be constant—at least until the third truth entered the picture. The first is Death."

"Ugh," said Sam.

"I know, I know. Well, we will all die, and that is a truth we can't change. And number two. Taxes. We will all pay taxes. We have been so conditioned that these are the two great truths that we think of them together."

"True," Jim said.

"Ok ready for the third great truth . . . drum roll please . . . Debt. There will always be debt. Does that shock you Sam?"

"I guess, yet I can see how that could be true. It is such a part of the economy and our day-to-day lives, so it makes sense. As I think about it, I can't envision a scenario where debt wouldn't exist."

"We want to plan for debt. Are you going to allow yourself to be affected by the government's debt? Do you have debt? If yes, is it good debt or bad debt?"

Kevin brought up a website www.usdebtclock.org to show and explain to Sam what the government debt and tax revenue looks like.

Sam leaned in to look.

"So, Sam, what you think is going to happen with taxes in the future? Do you think they will go up or down based on what you just saw?"

Sam replied, "I'm not sure how they *wouldn't* go up!"

"The government has a math problem. As with most math problems, only a couple of solutions seem to exist," Kevin said.

Jim chimed in and asked Sam, "Do you see how we, as business owners, need to go back to basics and follow the rules in **The Richest Man in Babylon** by shifting ourselves from a B Quadrant to an I Quadrant?"

"I do," Sam replied.

"Kevin, are you going to go through the Economic Termites?" Jim asked.

"Yes, we are at a good point to go over them and what they mean to Sam," Kevin said.

"Great," Sam said. "I'm curious what they are."

"Sam, I bet you are asking yourself about Economic Termites at this point!" Kevin laughed. "Why don't we begin by defining what it means? I developed this term to help create a visual of how certain economic terms, processes, and events affect us. Sam, what are termites?"

Sam felt a bit foolish having to explain what a termite was, but he played along. "They're bugs that eat wood."

"Right. They're called 'silent destroyers.' When do you know when you have a termite problem?"

Sam replied, "When the damage has been done, and when it's too late."

"Exactly. I know it felt funny answering such a simple question, but events in our business and personal lives have 'silent destroyers.' They can cause damage without us even knowing about it—until it's too late."

Sam furrowed his brow.

"It's okay, Sam, because we plan for these things. When talking about building assets and financial well-being, we need to review how certain events could cause harm to your plan of building assets. At this point I think it important to point out that we are essentially in the I Quadrant (Investor) of the *Cashflow Quadrant* while we build assets. Depending upon the plan and execution of the plan, building assets and certain assets causes us to enter both the S Quadrant (Self-Employed) and/or the B Quadrant (Business). Moving forward, you may hear me use the term 'business' or 'business owner' for that reason. Again, we want to enhance your B Quadrant and I Quadrant statuses, respectively."

Sam said, "I can see that. If assets generate income, then they would be starting a business of sorts. Aren't there ways to structure assets as a business?"

"Yes. Entity structuring and entity types are for another conversation, and we can discuss it as we get further along in the planning process."

"Got it," Sam said.

"Sam, did you notice earlier I said how 'events could cause harm to your plan of building assets'? In our opinion, you become a business owner due to asset building. As a business owner, you experience no separation between your 'business' life and your 'personal' life. When decisions are made in one area, they affect the other. Do you agree?"

"Yes absolutely! This is why we are talking isn't it?" Sam replied.

"Right. As business owners, we can compartmentalize certain aspects of our business and personal lives, yet each affects the other when we look at the big picture and have to make business decisions that affect our personal lives."

"I understand that!" Jim said.

"When you see pictures of how termites can cause damage without even knowing about it, you see that the exterior often remains intact while the termites have created holes on the interior. When the inside loses its strength, the outside façade deteriorates. The strength of your business is the integrity of the interior."

Jim chimed in and said, "You must be wondering what the Economic Termites are."

"Yes!"

Kevin pulled out a sheet that listed them. He said, "Our goal is to address the four major Economic Termites."

ECONOMIC
TERMITES

① TAXES

② INFLATION

③ TIME

④ LAWS/REGULATIONS

"We may touch on one or two of the others. Although we are focusing on the major four, it does not mean we do not address *all* the Economic Termites in our planning. In fact, by following the rules from *The Richest Man in Babylon*, we inherently plan for the majority of the Economic Termites."

"Before we go into these termites, we need to address some economic terms," Kevin said. He pulled out a sheet of the paper with the list:

1) Opportunity Cost.

2) Difference of Revenue vs Income vs Lifestyle Income vs Non-Lifestyle Income.

3) Expenses.

Sam read the three items on the sheet.

"Have you heard of these before?"

Sam answered, "Of course."

"The economic term Opportunity Costs crosses over into our business and personal lives. What does this mean to us? How does this affect your business of asset building? Simply put, we need to be mindful of what or where we spend our money, energy and time."

Sam nodded.

"Let me explain, let's say you decide to go to lunch with a group of friends to reminisce and talk about the old days. Alternately, you could attend training to learn about asset building that has the potential to help you reach that next level—or at least help you hit those goals you set."

"Okay," Sam said.

"You probably would have a great time with your friends. But what did you miss by not attending the training? How did not attending the training affect your business? We don't know if you would have ended up learning how to improve your business to hit those goals or not. We won't know if that training could have led you to an asset to become successful or achieve compounding or the moment of Velocity of Money sooner. You get the point! That's Opportunity Cost. Sam, what would you do in this scenario?"

OPPORTUNITY COST

OPPORTUNITY A

OPPORTUNITY B

"Well, Kevin, I believe it may depend on where the person's mind is at. For me, I am ready. Right now, I would choose the training. Before Jim and I met the other day, I probably would have chosen hanging with friends."

"I agree that timing plays a role. Now, we want to distinguish the difference between Revenue, Income, Lifestyle Income and Non-Lifestyle Income. You may know this already, but I want to make sure we are on the same page. First, cash flow is the net amount of cash and cash-equivalents being transferred into and out of a business. At the most fundamental level, a company's ability to create value for shareholders is determined by its ability to generate positive cash flows or, more specifically, maximize long-term free cash flow."

"This is all making sense," Sam said.

"Great! If you are a business, you need revenue to pay for expenses and that results in a profit or loss. Generating positive cash flow allows you to have long-term growth, so you want to limit taxable income within the guidelines laid out by the IRS. Often, people ask me the difference between revenue and income. When understanding the difference, we need to take a step back and dissect each term and where they should be placed."

TYPES OF INCOME

1. REVENUE (BUSINESS)
2. NET INCOME (BUSINESS)
3. INCOME
4. LIFESTYLE INCOME
5. NON-LIFESTYLE INCOME
6. CASH FLOW (BUSINESS)
7. TAXABLE INCOME (BUSINESS)

Sam took a look at what Kevin wrote.

"Sam, what is **revenue**?"

"The income generated by a business, which is also called earnings or gross profit," Sam replied.

"Correct. **Revenue is shown usually as the top item in an Income (profit and loss) Statement from which all charges, costs, and expenses are subtracted to arrive at** net income. At the bottom is the Net Income or Profit. Keep in mind each business expense, though it is an expense, provides tax savings as a business deduction. When businesses talk about income, they are usually referring to Revenue unless they are talking about "Net Income." In that case, they'll use the term income or profit/loss. For some non-business owners, this becomes confusing since most times the term "income" refers to income to the individual, which is different. This all makes sense, right?"

Sam answered, "Yes."

"Good. Then, let's talk about income. It's the flow of cash or cash-equivalents received from work (wages or salary), capital (interest or profit), or land (rent). For a business, this is an expense line item titled as Salaries and Wages on the 1040 personal federal tax return. For the individual, this is your personal balance sheet topline. If we were to use the example of a personal checking account, your personal expenses are subtracted from this balance in your checking account to create the new balance."

"Okay," Sam said.

"I want to make sure we understand this, because we're going to discuss what I call Lifestyle Income/Expenses. I use this term to indicate what your personal income is used for, usually your monthly expenses. Many times, this is referred to as a budget. In general, I dislike the term 'budget' because people view it negatively. **Lifestyle Income/Expenses should be what you spend your money on**. If you spend $500 a month on movies, then that is part of your Lifestyle Income/Expenses."

"That would be a LOT of movies," Sam said.

"True," Kevin replied. "And there's no judgment about how or where you spend your money. It's your money. At the end of the month, you may have discretionary income or leftover income used for savings."

"That sounds good, doesn't it?" Jim asked.

"Yes," Sam said. He was already looking more relaxed than when he arrived.

"Now I'm going to discuss **Non-Lifestyle Income**, which is that discretionary income not used as Lifestyle Income/Expenses. When we discuss taxes, we'll revisit these terms, so you can see how the planning process reveals Opportunity Costs associated with certain Lifestyle Income/Expenses and Non-Lifestyle Income.

Sam said, "I'm glad we went through this even though it's basic. It reinforced what I already know and shed light on how you view the basics to set up your planning."

"Great! As you know now, **taxes are an Economic Termite**. And I created a formula to communicate the tax savings opportunities."

Kevin wrote out the formula that leads to the Appreciable Deduction Planning process.

$$\frac{\begin{array}{l} AGI\ \$ \underline{\hspace{3cm}} \\ -\ LIFESTYLE\ \$ \underline{\hspace{3cm}} \\ INCOME \end{array}}{NON\text{-}LIFESTYLE\ \boxed{\$ \hspace{3cm}}}$$
$$INCOME$$

"Kevin, this formula makes sense, but how does this relate to your planning?"

"Well, when you ask your CPA questions about saving more on taxes, what do they tell you?"

Sam answered, "Usually, they say they have done everything they can, and we are going to just to pay the taxes owed."

"How does that make you feel?"

"It angers me," said Sam.

"It should. When you meet with an advisor or some other financial professional and you ask them how they can help you, nine times out of ten they tell you they can invest your money or get you this amount of rate of return. At times, they say you should write a check to invest in such and such, right?"

Sam replied, "Yes! There is no originality."

Kevin smiled. "Exactly. I would get frustrated, too. Because each time I met with a client, they would think I was going to do the same thing. **My formula shows you, based on *your* numbers, what amount of income you are paying taxes on that you said *wasn't needed* for your lifestyle.** You okay with me asking a few personal financial questions?"

"Ask away."

"Great. What is your AGI?" Kevin asked.

"$350,000."

"What do you spend on a monthly basis?" Kevin asked.

"Oh, I guess about $12,500 a month."

"Ok, so that's about $16,000 gross or $200,000 a year. When I subtract $200,000 from an AGI of $350,000, it equals $150,000 of Non-Lifestyle Income. So you are paying taxes on $150,000 a year you don't need as part of your monthly spending."

$$AGI \ \$350,000$$
$$- \ LIFESTYLE \ \$200,000$$
$$INCOME$$
$$\overline{NON\text{-}LIFESTYLE \ \$150,000}$$
$$INCOME$$

"Wow. What's that in dollars?" Sam asked.

"The majority of that income is in the 24% bracket, so let's just keep it simple. Get your phone out, and bring up your calculator."

Sam took his phone out.

"Okay. Type in 150,000 times point 24 (0.24). What does it say?"

Sam replied, "$36,000."

"I want you to do one more thing. Type in 150,000 again. This time, multiply that by point 093 (0.093). That is the California state bracket number. What's the answer?"

"13,950," Sam said.

"Last step, Sam. Add that number 13,950 plus the previous number of 36,000. What does that equal?"

"Ugh. 49,950. Don't tell me. That is what I'd owe in taxes, huh?" Sam said.

Kevin replied, "Yes, that is an estimate. So now you have a real number. What could you do with an extra 49,950 dollars? What do you think the IRS wants you to do with that extra money?"

Sam shook his head.

"We call this a liability, which is when you owe something to someone or something. In this case, both the Federal and State governments are owed money. For this, we use the term '*tax* liability.' Typically, we go through the tax brackets and explain how the brackets work, so you have an idea of what we are talking about when we begin our tax bracket management education."

Sam nodded again and put his phone down. "This is a lot to take in."

"I know it is. Jim probably felt the same way! This is a good spot to talk about the term 'Opportunity Cost.' I'd like to show you the Opportunity Cost you are facing right now. Would that be all right?"

Sam nodded yes.

As Kevin began to pull up the sheet to calculate the answer, Sam glanced at Jim with a look that seemed to say he couldn't believe what he'd been doing for so many years.

"Kevin, I have to say I'm a bit frustrated, because I have an idea you are going to be driving home the idea of tax planning, so I don't keep giving money away. I understand now after you talked about the IRS and compared the guidelines to a GPS or map, of sorts, and which give us the chance to save."

[**Author note**: *In section one, I wrote how we want to find our "tax planning GPS." If we want to drive from point A to point B, we'd used a map or GPS. Let's say that GPS or map represents the IRS Tax Code. We have choices on how to travel from point A to B. The GPS guides us. When we encounter a detour, the GPS helps us navigate around it. When it comes to taxes, you want to find your tax planning GPS to navigate the "route" efficiently. See chapter 1 for more.*]

"Yes, the IRS is smart. They want you to use the map. And I want you to see in numbers what is at stake. So you are looking at one year of savings. We did a plan and you only saved one year's worth of taxes, which is the $49,950. Since you are 55 years old, I entered your age here and assumed you plan to "retire" at age 65. We don't use the term "retirement," because that term was created to entice us to save money for a certain age. As pension plans go away, the retirement conversation focuses on social security, which begins at age 65. Banks and insurance companies began to focus on how people need to save for their retirement at that age. That created this mindset that people had to stop working at age 65. Rather than talk about retirement, we help people understand we're building assets for when we want to shift our lifestyle to taking income from assets and not worry so much about our work income."

"Interesting," Sam said.

"We need to look at a ten-year period in which we assume five percent appreciation of that original $49,950 compounds to $81,363."

1 YEAR
―――――――――

$49,950
        10 YRS
         5 %.
―――――――――
$81,363

"But keep in mind that the plans we incorporate are for every year, so the next calculation shows a savings every year for ten years at the same five percent appreciation.

EVERY YEAR
―――――――――

$49,950
        10 YRS
         5%.
―――――――――
$628,266

"Now, Sam, wouldn't you agree this is a good deal?"

Sam furrowed his brow in confusion. "Well, no, not for me. For the IRS, this a great deal."

Kevin smiled.

"Ah, you are being sarcastic," Sam said.

They laughed.

"Kevin, your explanation of the E and S Quadrants is coming back to me. You said the IRS gives businesses the ability to save on taxes, so they can hire employees. I'm a business owner, and I am basically sticking it to myself as an employee. I forget that I wear two hats as both employee and owner."

"Great job, Sam! You have taken a huge step from the employee mindset to the business owner mindset. Now you understand why I have been guiding you through this process."

"Yes. I do now," Sam said.

"You have to come to the realization that you are not an employee. You are a business owner first. I want to show you the Opportunity Cost associated with the $150,000 that is your Non-Lifestyle Income. Using the same formula, we now see that the $150,000 appreciates to $244,334.

1 YEAR
$150,000
      10 YRS
      5%
$244,334

"As we plan for each year over the next ten years, the savings grows to $1,886,684. Now the question is how much of this savings would you want income tax free?"

EVERY YEAR
$150,000
      10 YRS
      5%
$1,886,684

Sam laughed. "What kind of question is that!? Of course, I would want *all* of it to be income tax free! But that isn't possible is it?"

Kevin replied, "Before I answer that question I'd like to go through some more education and have you answer that question. Fair enough?"

"Ok," Sam said.

"I am going to show you the Income Funnel. This funnel gives you a visual of how income flows from your various income streams. Along the top, you have your income, and it flows down the funnel. Where do you think the income flows to?"

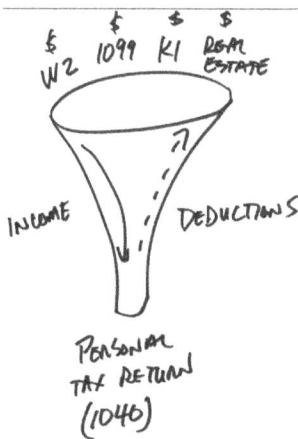

"I guess to me."

"Yes, that's right. Let's take it a step further. How does the IRS know you have income?"

"My tax return?" Sam asked.

"Exactly right. When all your income flows down the

funnel to your tax return, what do we call that total income number?"

"Kevin, are you trying to be funny? That's my AGI, my adjusted gross income."

"I'm not trying to be funny. I just want to make sure you understand this part, because this is the backbone to the formula and what gives you hope with saving on taxes. You understand the opportunity cost with this plan. When we do our planning, we shift your Non-Lifestyle Income back up the Income Funnel to your business through the corporate return. Does that make sense?"

"Yes. So which deduction do we use? Because my CPA said more than once that we have no other options to save on taxes. He has said I should feel good I have income to be taxed. Each time I hear that, I become so mad. I don't show it, because I know he is doing what he can. He wouldn't purposely not save money on taxes."

Kevin replied, "You are right. Your CPA is doing the best he can. He's doing what he has been trained to do. Look at it from his perspective. He has the entire tax code to know. Let's go back to our map analogy. Do you know anyone who knows the entire map and which road to take at which time?"

"Of course not," Sam said.

"That's why GPS makes our lives easier," Kevin said.

"The computer does all the heavy lifting. Your CPA has more individual tax returns to do than business returns. So you need someone who knows the business side of the map to help your CPA. At the end of the day, who signs your tax returns?"

Sam replied, "I do."

"That's right. So you are responsible no matter which GPS you use. When we are talking about those deductions for businesses, we have to look at the two types of deductions.

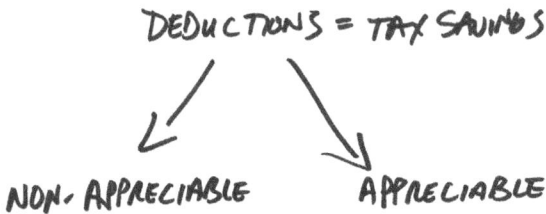

DEDUCTIONS = TAX SAVINGS

NON-APPRECIABLE   APPRECIABLE

"Non-Appreciable deductions include office supplies, office furniture, or even the company vehicle you lease. These represent a tax savings, because the IRS gives us the ability to subtract the Expenses from our Revenue. These Expenses represent a deduction, which represents tax savings. We don't have to pay income tax on the expenses. Does that makes sense?"

"Yes," Sam answered.

"Great. Now, if the universe is balanced and we have up and down, right and left, forward and backward, male and female, yes and no, then we probably have an opposite for Non-Appreciable Deduction. What would you say it is?"

Sam laughed and said, "Appreciable."

"Jim didn't tell you there was going to be test question did he?" Kevin said, smiling.

"Ha," Sam replied.

"Appreciable Deductions are deductions that represent tax savings. Since they have the opportunity to appreciate in value, they can be worth more a year from now than the original deduction. Makes sense, doesn't it?"

"Yes," said Sam.

"As a business owner, would you prefer a Non-Appreciable Deduction or an Appreciable Deduction?"

Sam replied, "Kevin, I'm wondering why I'm only learning all this now?"

Kevin answered, "I don't have an answer other than to say that at least you are now. But I do have a question for you. Why is it important to understand that there are Appreciable Deductions?"

"Because there are other Economic Termites?"

"That's right. The next Economic Termite is Inflation. So trying to use our tax savings to appreciate allows us to try and stay ahead of inflation. In our firm, we discuss inflation from an expense-based planning position versus an income-based position. Think back to the story of a horse called Income. Remember, the cart "Expenses" is what Income pulled. Towards the end, Income couldn't pull the cart because the Expenses became too heavy, so we had to add another horse called Second Income."

"Right," Sam said.

"What happens with inflation? Let's say that expenses didn't increase due to spending. Eventually, Inflation causes the expenses to increase. When it comes to assets, we call it 'appreciation,' and we call it 'inflation' when it comes to expenses. Inflation over the last 30 years averaged 2.65%. Our $200,000 in expenses over a ten-year period, assuming five percent appreciation, means that same $200,000 is valued at $259,788."

Kevin wrote this all down and showed it to Sam and Jim.

EXPENSE BASED
PLANNING
_____
$ 200,000
10 YRS
2.65 %
_____
$259, 788

"Over a 30 year period, the $200,000 becomes $438,327!

$$\frac{\begin{array}{r} \$200,000 \\ 30 \text{ YRS} \\ 2.65 \% \end{array}}{\$438,327}$$

"Wow," Sam said.

"The Rule of 72 explaines how we can predict when inflation or any asset can double in value. Have you heard of it before?"

"I don't think so. It sounds familiar."

"Don't worry about it. Most people haven't. The calculation is simple. You take the number 72 and divide it by the interest rate or the assumed appreciation rate. Let's use the inflation number of 2.65%."

Once again, Kevin wrote down the example to illustrate his point.

$$\frac{\text{RULE OF } 72}{2.65 \overline{)\ 72}} \quad 27 \text{ YRS}$$

"Based on the rule of 72, it will take 27 years for the inflation number of 2.65% to cause our expenses to double. As you can see, you need your income to increase. As a business owner, increased income means a possible increase in income taxes even if tax brackets don't increase. The rules in *The Richest Man in Babylon* become important to understanding the *Cashflow Quadrant*. Knowing how income works and is taxed forces us to understand the rules to assets. Since assets are what income is generated from, we want to make sure we have control of the income. Do you see how it all is connected?"

Sam sat there amazed.

Jim laughed. He'd been quiet for a long time. Frankly, Sam had never seen his brother not speak for so long.

Sam said, "I see it and wonder if there is anything we can do now?"

Jim grew serious. "It is almost never too late. Remember, the word 'retirement' doesn't exist when building assets. Main Financial Distributors include banks, investment companies, and insurance companies, and they create products for salespeople to sell. Basically, they sell financial products. These Main Financial Distributors want us to think retirement is important and to put a time limit on it, so we act now to save for it. And that's just so they can sell products and services to the masses, including us!"

"I didn't think about that before," Sam said.

"You are a business owner and not an employee. You wear two hats, so you need to view this from a business owner perspective. Let me ask you a question. Do you want to sell your business or close the doors?"

Sam replied, "Not as of now. I haven't thought about it."

Jim responded, "That's the exact point. Business owners don't think about it. We don't think of 'retirement' unless someone hounds us enough to make us think and act. We want to build assets to control our future. By following rule number seven in *The Richest Man in Babylon*— increase your ability to earn—then we don't have to save for 'retirement.' Instead, we build assets."

"Ah, ok," Sam said.

"You see, Sam, I'm a business owner, because I don't have to be an employee and have others tell me what to do. Do you see why we build assets? To put the power in your hands," Kevin said.

"I get it," Sam replied.

"The Rule of 72 helps us estimate how long before your money can double. To find out how long, you take the rate of return and divide it into 72. The result is the number of years it would take for your money to double."

Kevin showed this calculation to Sam to show him it would take 14.4 years for his money to double with a 5% rate of return.

$$5\overline{)72}\quad 14.4\text{ yrs}$$

"We want to follow rule number three from *The Richest Man in Babylon*, which is to earn a fair rate of return. If we know inflation could double over 27 years, and we have assets that appreciate at an estimated five percent, then we could have our assets doubling in 14.4 years. The same five percent over 14.4 years means our asset could reach $800,000, which is almost double the inflation number. Back to our issue: taxable income.

$$
\begin{array}{ll}
1 & \$\,200{,}000 \\
14.4 & \$\,400{,}000 \\
28.8 & \$\,800{,}000
\end{array}
$$

"We can put control of the future in our hands. At a basic five percent appreciation, and without taking undo risk, we could allow our assets to double. What if all this money was taxable income, would you think it could last long with taxes and inflation?"

"No," said Sam.

"Let me draw this out in a basic diagram to show you." Kevin took a pen and drew a chart for Sam.

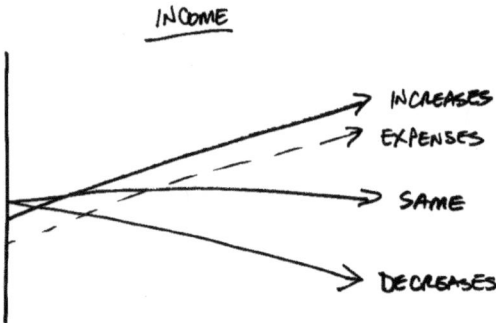

INCOME

INCREASES
EXPENSES
SAME
DECREASES

"If this is your income, you have choices about how you want your income distributed from your assets. If your income stays the same, look at the line that says 'same.' Since we just discussed inflation, look at the dotted line 'expenses.' Even though you began with lower expenses due to inflation, your expenses surpass your income if left the same. If we have inflation and your expenses are increasing, then your income can't stay the same. That means you have to look at the line 'decreases.' Based on this, you have to have your income increase, so look at the line 'increases.'"

Sam shook his head in wonder. Kevin had more questions.

"What do you want to do with this information, Sam?"

Sam knew this information was basic. He still felt a bit mad, because he hadn't been planning this way fifteen years ago.

"Can I be honest with you, Kevin?"

"Please. You can always be honest with me. We are talking about your money and future."

"Kevin, I'm mad and frustrated. I'm feeling like the time has passed for me to do anything like what you just explained. You made this seem basic and like something I should have been doing for the last decade or so. Please understand you didn't say that or make me feel like that. That's just what my mind is telling me."

Kevin leaned closer to listen.

"I look at all the money I squandered away—the money lost in investments, taxes I have paid. The list goes on. I'm looking at your list of the rules in *The Richest Man in Babylon*, and I failed at them."

Jim spoke up, "Sam. Remember Kevin said there is no timeline. There is no 'retirement' age you need to hit. You are thinking like an employee, which is not what you are. You are a business owner, and you need to think like one. Kevin said you, as an owner, have the ability to use the IRS code to your advantage. You just need to find the right GPS. You can use your business to jump start this and enhance the compounding."

Sam didn't look completely convinced.

"Look at it from a big picture perspective. If you do this now, you will put your business in a better financial position, which is what the IRS wants you to do. So when the economy goes through its cycle, and experiences a downturn, you will be in a position not to have to layoff employees. You can keep them. In fact, Kevin explained to me how we can keep our same good customer service or improve it during such downturns, because our competition isn't financially prepared. That means you can begin taking over market share."

"Hmm," Sam said. Jim could tell he was thinking hard about this.

"Your business will leap frog the competition, and your business asset will compound. That causes the rest of the asset-building plan to compound, too," Jim said.

Kevin listened to them talk.

Sam looked over at Kevin and asked, "So based on what Jim just said, **this is where the third Economic Termite comes in? Time.**"

Kevin finally spoke up, "Yes. Your frustrations are valid, and many of my business owner clients had similar feelings. Your frustration about time lost is probably the best explanation of time. I can expand, but you did a better job than I could.

"**The fourth Economic Termite is Laws and Regulations**. This termite often angers my clients. We have been discussing the IRS and taxes, but I learned that most laws passed had some sort of consequence to the tax code. As tax payers, we either received some sort of benefit or some sort of penalty. The lawmakers have realized we respond to the passing of laws or voting down laws based on the taxes."

"Here is my disclaimer: I am not getting political here. Both sides of the aisle are guilty of using the tax code to their advantage. Let's look at one major law that changed. But before we begin, let's look at what the word 'regulation' means. '*Rule based on and meant to carry out a specific piece of legislation. Regulations are enforced usually by a regulatory agency formed or mandated to carry out the purpose or provisions of a legislation.*' The Federal Registry is the main source to track the various regulations. In fact, I read that, 'in 1936, the number of pages in the Federal Register was about 2,600. Today, the Federal Register is over 80,000 pages long.'"

"That's longer than I would have guessed," Sam said.

"Exactly. Here are a couple examples of how silly some of these are." Kevin handed Sam a sheet of paper with this list.

- *The city of Philadelphia now requires all bloggers to purchase a $300 business privilege license.*

- *The state of Louisiana says that monks must be fully licensed as a funeral directors and actually convert their monasteries into a licensed funeral homes before they will be allowed to sell their handmade wooden caskets.*

- *In the state of Massachusetts, all children in day-care centers are mandated by state law to brush their teeth after lunch. In fact, the state even provides the fluoride toothpaste for the children.*

- *If you attempt to give a tour of our nation's capital without a license, you could be put in prison for 90 days.*

As the guys were sitting there laughing, Kevin continued.

"I know these are ridiculous. I'm trying to poke fun at some of them. But why are they even wasting paper and tax payers' time for these? Okay, Sam, one example of a law that caused significant change was Obamacare. We heard that taxes would not be increased. Of course, those with a brain wondered how the country would pay for this. The answer? Taxes. According to Americans for Tax Reform[29] there were 20 changes."

Kevin pulled out a piece of paper and showed Sam and Jim the various laws and regulations that were used to pay for this new law. (To see this list in more detail go to section 1 of this book.)

1. Obamacare Individual Mandate Excise Tax

2. Obamacare Employer Mandate Tax

3. Obamacare Surtax on Investment Income

4. Obamacare Excise Tax on Comprehensive Health Insurance Plans

5. Obamacare Hike in Medicare Payroll Tax

6. Obamacare Medicine Cabinet Tax

7. Obamacare HSA Withdrawal Tax Hike

8. Obamacare Flexible Spending Account Cap—aka "Special Needs Kids Tax"

9. Obamacare Tax on Medical Device Manufacturers)

10. Obamacare "Haircut" for Medical Itemized Deduction from 7.5% to 10% of AGI

11. Obamacare Tax on Indoor Tanning Services

12. Obamacare elimination of tax deduction for employer-provided retirement Rx drug coverage in coordination with Medicare Part D

13. Obamacare Blue Cross/Blue Shield Tax Hike

14. Obamacare Excise Tax on Charitable Hospitals

15. Obamacare Tax on Innovator Drug Companies

16. Obamacare Tax on Health Insurers

17. Obamacare $500,000 Annual Executive Compensation Limit for Health Insurance Executives

18. Obamacare Employer Reporting of Insurance on W-2

19. Obamacare "Black liquor" tax hike

20. Obamacare Codification of the "economic substance doctrine"

Sam spoke up, "Kevin I'm not surprised by this, but I *am* surprised as to the extent the changes occurred. We didn't hear about any of this."

Kevin agreed, "We didn't. Are you surprised? Did your health insurance premiums go up or down? What has been the average health care cost increase been since Obamacare took effect?"

"Up," said Sam.

"That's why Laws and Regulations are part of the Economic Termites list. Think of how many rules from *The Richest Man of Babylon* this one law affected."

Jim spoke up, "Kevin, can you talk about some of the other possible changes that have been talked about over the years? Sam, I found this to be more eye opening, and it could be the sole reason why anyone should hire Kevin and his firm."

Kevin responded, "Sure, Jim. Back in 2017, according to the *LA Times*, one of the areas discussed was removing the tax deductibility of 401(k) plans.[30] Back in 2014, according to CNBC,[31] President Obama was discussing removing some of the benefits of 401(k) plans."

Sam said, "WHAT!!!"

Kevin pulled out a couple quotes by President Obama.

> *"Under Obama's budget plan, higher-income earners would be limited to a tax deduction at the 28 percent level, even if their current income-tax bracket is much higher.*
>
> *If this budget actually becomes law, a person who is at the highest marginal tax bracket of 39.6 percent (this doesn't include state income taxes or the 3.8 percent Obamacare tax) would only be entitled to a tax deduction equal to those individuals in the 28 percent tax bracket."*

Kevin explained, "This did not happen. But some are for it. What could this mean to Americans who have been told over the last two to three decades to save in these retirement accounts? According to Investment Company Institute,[32] 'as of December 31, 2017 401(k) plans held an estimated $5.3 trillion in assets and represented 19 percent of the $27.9 trillion in US retirement assets.' What would happen if Congress decided to have a special income tax on retirement assets when they are distributed as income? What if they decided that income from an approved retirement account will receive an excise tax of 5% in addition to federal tax brackets?"

"That would not be good," Sam said.

"What could you and I do? Let's look at this math. We multiply the assets of $27.9 trillion by five percent and that equals a total tax potential of $1.395 trillion dollars. Could the federal government use this extra tax revenue? Do you think the states would also jump on this bandwagon and create their own retirement tax, too?"

Jim nodded. He knew what was coming next.

"Sam, I'm going to bring up a website www.usdebtclock.org. I want to review with you our national debt and the revenue. You remember our earlier discussion of this."

As they talked back and forth about the frustrating things about politics and government, they concluded Sam had to take action.

"One more topic for today—the three financial distributors." Kevin wrote them out.

BANK = LEVERAGE

INVESTMENT COMPANIES = RISK

INSURANCE COMPANIES = SAFETY

"Banks represent leverage. That means banks make their money by using other people's money to make money. Personal or business deposits go into the bank. The bank must hold at least 10% of that deposit. The remainder can be loaned out (leverage) in the form of loans of all kinds, including credit cards. Now investment companies represent risk, which means that they make their money off fees or spreads of investments. To keep this simple, do you have any mutual funds?"

Sam replied, "Yes. We have some in a brokerage account."

Kevin continued, "Have you ever read the prospectus? Don't answer that because everyone says 'No.' Look at the prospectus or go onto the mutual fund's website, and it will say the following."

Kevin pulled out a sheet of paper, which he had Sam read.

"All investing is subject to risk, including the possible loss of the money you invest. Past performance is no guarantee of future results. Be aware that fluctuations in the financial markets and other factors may cause declines in the value of your account. There is no guarantee that any particular asset allocation or mix of funds will meet your investment objectives or provide you with a given level of income. Diversification does not ensure a profit or protect against a loss.

"The performance data shown represent past performance, which is not a guarantee of future results. Investment returns and principal value will fluctuate, so that investors' shares, when sold, may be worth more or less than their original cost. Current performance may be lower or higher than the performance data cited."

Kevin sat there waiting for Sam to say something.

Sam spoke up and said, "That seems pretty clear. The money is at risk, and I could lose money. The funny thing is I knew that. After reading it aloud, why does it sound so bad? I know I'm taking a risk, and I know I could lose some of my money. But, for whatever reason, I'm not comfortable with what I read."

"Sam, why do you think that is?" Kevin asked.

Sam replied, "Well, I think because now it seems real. I know I am a business owner, and there is risk in that, but I can control that risk. At least, I feel as if I have more control."

Jim spoke up, "Sam it is because you don't want to lose your money. It's your money. When you read what your mutual fund says, you find you are relying on someone to have that control. I felt the same way. In fact, I immediately thought of 2008 and the early 2000s when everyone lost money."

Kevin said, "Your feelings and what you said are valid,

so that's why the third financial distributor is Insurance Companies. They represent safety. In fact, every state has an insurance commission responsible for the compliance and monitoring of the insurance companies and industry. All the state commissioners come together to represent the National Association of Insurance Commissioners (NAIC). They develop guidelines for across state lines. According to their website, the State of California requires the insurance company to have at least 100% in surplus for every dollar in insurance "capital," because insurance policies are a contract between you and the company. They must fulfill their duty as long as you fulfill yours. Let me ask you both a question, when it comes to Banks and Investment Companies, who is more obligated to perform in that relationship you or them?"

Sam responded, "If you are asking whether a contract with the bank is in my benefit or theirs, I would probably say theirs. Yes, they lend me money, but it's not their money. It's other people's money. I'm paying them an interest rate for that money, and most loans have the ability to be called before the term negotiated."

"With Investment Companies, we just read what their obligation is, so you need to make sure your current assets aren't too deep in one of these distributors. View their products as tools to meet your planning needs. You shouldn't be concerned with what a product is called but with what it does. Does that make sense?" Kevin asked.

Sam and Jim both nodded their heads.

Sam looked at his watch and said, "Oh man, I need to get going. Kevin, I'm convinced. I need to prepare for this war."

Kevin laughed. "There is battle to be won. We can only try and control your positioning with the mindset that we will still be affected by the Economic Termites. We plan to prepare and protect your assets through the planning process."

Sam added, "Kevin, I need to do this. How much are you going to charge me? I feel guilty asking this, because the amount of information you shared opened my eyes. I know this will be expensive. Based on what the alternative is, the Opportunity Costs, I have to say it is going to be worth it."

Kevin replied with a smile and a chuckle, "Sam, good use of Opportunity Costs. You're right about all of that. But it will only be expensive if you don't do anything. Here is what I do. Send me some information, and I'll do basic calculations of your specific situation and show you an overview of a possible plan. Based on that, we can discuss fees for implementing the plan. Even though I brought value to this conversation, I want to show you value based on your situation. I want to earn your business first before you agree to pay me. Fair?"

Sam replied, "That sounds fair.

SECTION THREE

How Strategy Layers Protect You and Your Business

The strategies we build for our clients protect them and look similar to an oak tree. An oak is solid, strong and massive. Maybe, as a child, you asked a teacher or parent the age of a massive tree. They explained how you could tell the tree's age by the rings on the inside and that each ring represents a year of growth. Our planning method is similar, yet we view each ring as strength and protection—not as years. Each ring represents the tree becoming stronger and stronger. (Please see the picture below to the right.)

The center represents the beginning, a sapling that's still small and weak. In the center, we're not yet protected from the environment. We add a protective ring when we start our business and set ourselves up as a corporation. Next, you find out you need insurance. Another layer is added, and it further insulates you from the environment. Each strategy we implement adds another ring to create more strength to protect you.

By reading this book, you've taken a definitive step toward improving your financial outcome. Thank you for reading *Economic Termites*. This book has been in the making for a long time. And I didn't release it until I felt we had a complete story to tell rather than just a chapter that left you to figure out the rest on your own.

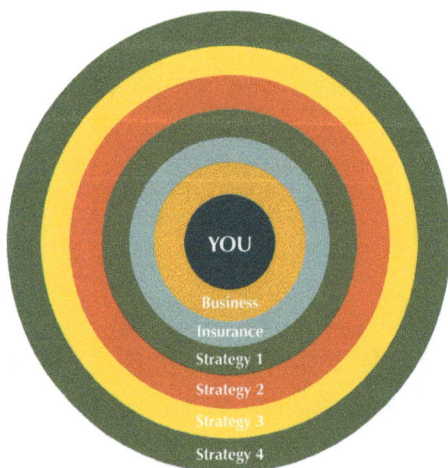

YOU
Business
Insurance
Strategy 1
Strategy 2
Strategy 3
Strategy 4

And now?

You have the opportunity to take another step.

Like Sam, you have a decision to make.

Some questions to ask yourself:

1) Do I feel like I am paying too much in taxes?

2) Do I feel like I could upgrade my GPS system when it comes to the road map of taxes?

3) Do I believe taxes will go up?

4) Have I been planning for inflation?

5) Do I feel like I need to plan for inflation?

6) Am I concerned about the time I could lose if I don't change?

7) Do I believe there will be laws and regulations that will pass or change that could negatively affect my livelihood?

8) Am I building assets?

9) Am I building the right assets?

10) Do I have a plan for my assets to work in unison with each other to reach the Velocity of Money?

11) Am I following the rules according to *The Richest Man in Babylon?*

12) Where am I on the *Cashflow Quadrant?*

13) Where do I want to be on the *Cashflow Quadrant?*

14) Are my assets working together to enhance my compounding potential?

And understand now the Opportunity Cost of not taking action.

If you need more time or education, you can join our membership site www.terrafirmamembers.com to receive more training about what has been discussed in this book.

Note: Please be advised we do not provide any advice until you engage our services. Since we do not know who you are or your situation, we can't begin to tell you what is possible. We don't want to make the mistake others in our industry make when they give the same recommendations to everyone without considering whether or not you'd be a good candidate for that strategy or plan.

REFERENCES

1   https://www.orkin.com/termites/

2   https://www.investopedia.com/terms/c/cfo.asp

3   https://www.investopedia.com/terms/c/cashflow.asp

4   https://www.dictionary.com/browse/educated

5   https://www.investopedia.com/ask/answers/12/what-is-an-asset.asp

6   http://www.richdad.com/resources/rich-dad-financial-education-blog/
    august-2013/the-worst-way-to-invest-your-retirement-money

7   https://www.investopedia.com/terms/c/compounding.asp

8   http://www.businessdictionary.com/definition/opportunity-cost.html

9   http://www.businessdictionary.com/definition/revenue.html

10 http://www.businessdictionary.com/definition/income.html

11 https://www.irs.gov/e-file-providers/definition-of-adjusted-gross-income

12 https://turbotax.intuit.com/tax-tips/irs-tax-return/what-is-adjusted-gross-
    income-agi/L2C6rCEit

13 http://www.businessdictionary.com/definition/liability.html

14 https://www.investopedia.com/terms/t/tax-deduction.asp

15 http://www.businessdictionary.com/definition/inflation.html

16 http://www.usinflationcalculator.com/frequently-asked-questions-faqs/

17 https://www.bls.gov/cpi/questions-and-answers.htm#Question_1

18 https://www.investopedia.com/terms/r/ruleof72.asp

19 http://www.usinflationcalculator.com/inflation/historical-inflation-rates/

20 https://en.wikipedia.org/wiki/Time

21 https://www.huffingtonpost.com/noah-st-john/why-procrastina-tion-is-th_b_7854176.html

22 https://globalwealthprotection.com/know-double-penny-day-analogy/

23 http://www.businessdictionary.com/definition/regulation.html

24 http://www.businessinsider.com/ridiculous-regulations-big-govern-ment-2010-11?slop=1#

25 https://www.atr.org/full-list-ACA-tax-hikes-a6996

26 http://www.latimes.com/business/hiltzik/la-fi-hiltzik-401k-taxes-20171023-story.html

27 https://www.cnbc.com/2014/03/18/obamas-budget-bad-for-401k-savers.html

28 https://www.ici.org/policy/retirement/plan/401k/faqs_401k

29 https://www.atr.org/full-list-ACA-tax-hikes-a6996

30 http://www.latimes.com/business/hiltzik/la-fi-hiltzik-401k-taxes-20171023-story.html

31 https://www.cnbc.com/2014/03/18/obamas-budget-bad-for-401k-savers.html

32 https://www.ici.org/policy/retirement/plan/401k/faqs_401k